More COMMON Sense

9 Things That Must Be Changed
In Order To Prevent
The
Collapse of America

KEN ENGLISH

WestBow
PRESS
A DIVISION OF THOMAS NELSON

WestBow Press books may be ordered through booksellers or by contacting:

WestBow Press
A Division of Thomas Nelson
1663 Liberty Drive
Bloomington, IN 47403
www.westbowpress.com
1 (866) 928-1240

ISBN: 978-1-4908-1073-7 (sc)
ISBN: 978-1-4908-1074-4 (hc)
ISBN: 978-1-4908-1072-0 (e)

Library of Congress Control Number: 2013918349

Printed in the United States of America.

WestBow Press rev. date: 10/22/2013

TABLE OF CONTENTS

DEDICATION

First to my loving wife Patsy: You are the only angel I know who resides fulltime on planet Earth. You were my high-school sweetheart and are now a dedicated wife who has stood by me as I searched for my niche in life. You've been a preacher's wife, coach's wife and now the wife of an entrepreneur, writer/rancher.

To the Late Reverend Alfred Ikner: You introduced me to Joseph and Mary's boy, Jesus Christ, and that has made all the difference in my life. He forgave me for the trash in my basket, and taught me how to forgive others when they throw trash in my basket.

To my daughter Jennifer, and son Kyle: You are both so special. Life would not be nearly as fun and interesting without you. Thanks for the wonderful grandchildren.

To Jason and Kaci: You are the best. God could not have sent us better partners for our children.

To the next generation of the English family: Ayden, Skye and Laken English; Davin, Dylan, and Daxton McCoy; May you all have a free and Christian America in which to grow up. May you grow in knowledge, wisdom, grace, and love of God and country.

To my sisters, Lorene and Elaine: Without you, red wagons, B.B. guns, county fairs, bicycles and Biscaynes would not have been part of my growing up experience.

To my incredible niece Debbie: Life has given you so many lemons; but you have learned to make great lemonade! Without your typing and computer skills, this book would still lie somewhere in the figment of my imagination.

A **special thanks** to Judy Dismukes who found time between caring for elderly parents and grandchildren to translate my red-neck country drawl into readable king's English.

Finally, to Ben McGee who encouraged the writing of this book and completed the final editing in record time, I offer my sincere appreciation for a job well done.

INTRODUCTION

It was the best of towns it was the worst of towns. Thus begins the story of an American patriot who wants to save America and the freedoms and privileges for which so many of our fellow countrymen have fought and died. The town I speak of is Gantt, Alabama. Well, maybe at that time, Gantt was not really a town. It had no mayor, no sheriff or traffic light. Nevertheless, Gantt is on the Alabama state map, a tiny dot, just east of Georgiana, where Hank Williams spun his lovesick ballads, drank whiskey and drove fast cars. It lies southwest of Dozier, from where Mal Moore, one of "Bear's" boys, hailed.

I was born about five miles outside of town. The muddy waters of the Patsaliga River flowed slowly to the Gulf of Mexico a few miles east of our house; and on the west side of our homestead, a thick piney woods owned by Judge Brogden shaded our front porch from the evening sun.

I arrived to take my place on the third rock from the sun on a bitterly cold January night in 1953. January 27, 1953 was an ordinary night in an ordinary week of an ordinary month in an ordinary year. It was a perfect time for the birth of an ordinary boy.

Neither Ford nor Chevrolet delivered an exceptional model that year. Thus, it was a year of ordinary boys and ordinary cars. Maybe if my parents had waited another couple of years, I could have been introduced to the world along with the classic 55 Chevy and 55 Thunderbird, and I too, might have been a classic collectible. As it was, I think my dad on seeing me for the first time, said; "throw him back! We'll wait and get a 55 model." I do not think the doctor who delivered me was too impressed either. Rumor has it, that instead of spanking me, he wanted to spank my mom for bringing such mayhem into an otherwise peaceful world.

Mark Twain's birth in 1835 was accompanied by a scheduled arrival of Halley's Comet which prompted Twain's mother to proclaim that this pre-mature and sickly boy would dazzle the world in a similar fashion as the icy heavenly visitor does on rare occasions. As for me, no celestial event heralded my birth—not even a solar flare or lunar eclipse. Nevertheless, after my encounter with Jesus, I have subscribed to the idea that an extraordinary God could somehow use an ordinary fellow like me if I would follow His directions.

My father and grandfather were tenant farmers or sharecroppers as some would refer to them. Neither of them had been educated beyond grammar school. My dad was also a construction worker, but when jobs were scarce and wild game even scarcer, he would resort to boot-legging to feed the family. The houses we lived in as I grew up were plain wood frame structures that the Big Bad Wolf could blow away with only two huffs and a puff. We never had to wonder about the health of our chickens because we could see them through the cracks in the floor. We had no worries about the septic tank running over or the commode not flushing, for these items were only for city folks. I was eighteen years old before I realized that I could take care of business without getting bitten on the butt by a spider, getting an occasional splinter in the rump from the rough boards that formed the toilet seat, or clean up afterwards with something other than a corncob or a worn out Sears catalog. Given the circumstances, I was as happy as any one of the Waltons or Clampets.

I did not have many things that others might have possessed, and at the time I was probably envious or jealous. Time and maturity have taught me the true value of the things that I did have. I recall that I never did have one of those square tin lunch boxes with a picture of the Lone Ranger on the outside, and a thermos on the inside. My sisters and I used what we had, which usually consisted of an empty syrup can which worked pretty good; we just couldn't put a square sandwich made from store-bought light bread in the round syrup can without mangling our sandwich. This was all right because we rarely had any store-bought bread. What we did have in good supply was momma's "cat-head" biscuits, which were more or less round and fit into the can perfectly. With my next stimulus money from Obama I plan to buy not one but a whole collection of metal lunch boxes from the Lone Ranger to Mickey Mouse.

My parents and teachers made sure that I never hungered for food or knowledge. My early teachers instilled in me a dynamic sense of patriotism, love, and loyalty to our great country. We would always start the days with prayer, the Pledge of Allegiance, and on many occasions, a patriotic song. I was so patriotic that on those rare occasions that I did go to town, I would salute a barber pole or anything that was red, white, and blue. I would get furious when I saw someone throw litter on the streets, roads, or rivers. I still remember seeing that commercial on TV where an old Indian sheds tears after seeing the land he loved being polluted.

I am like that old Indian and am angered today by a far worse pollution—the pollution of politics. I did not know or care much about politics in those early days growing up in south Alabama. My dad never spoke to me of politics; in fact, we did not discuss much of anything, not even baseball.

I reckon I knew we had freedom of speech since my mom never got arrested for the brutal and eloquent "cussins" she heaped on dad when he would show up drunk and disorderly or if we had to go retrieve him and his empty wallet from some beer joint. I realized that we had the right to "bear arms" because my dad's hunting skills provided most of the meat on our table. He was a good shot, even when slightly under the influence. I also became very aware that these rights and freedoms did have limits and boundaries. The Alabama version of the Federal Revenuers raided our tranquil little tenant farm one cool October day in 1963. I was only ten years old; President John F. Kennedy was about to be assassinated in a short while and I was about to be indoctrinated into the wild world of a game called "hide the whiskey before the law finds it." While the Revenuers were at the front door, my mom rushed me out the back door with two gallons of Papa's premium elixir. I had instructions to put it where the sun didn't shine, in other words, under the seat of the outhouse. The plan worked like a charm as the pungent odor of the privy deterred the posse from searching the outhouse.

The motivation for writing this book will become more and more apparent as I relate a few more memorable incidents from my childhood. Rawls High School, which had only six students in its last graduating class, like our house, did not have indoor plumbing when I first went there in 1959. However, Rawls was a great school with great teachers. This place was, and always shall be, dear to my heart for the lifetime friendships which began there and the education received in those classrooms where the only air-conditioning was an open window. Those fine ladies taught much more than the 3 Rs. They may have been a little slack in supervision at recess because a few of us boys would play in the woods a half mile from the school and way beyond the scrutiny of our mentors. Let me repeat: They were not slack in teaching us the academic disciplines and respect for God and fellow man. I learned that the rights and freedoms which we all enjoyed were like our salvation, "bought with a great price." Many of the fights I engaged in as a young lad were fought defending the rights of a weaker kid against bullies. Then as now, I consider it my duty as a southern gentleman to defend the rights of others against bullies and tyrants and to come to the rescue of any institution that I think is being threatened by injustice or menace of any kind. Today, bullies from without and ungodly corruption and socialism from within are threatening America. I am ready to take on the bullies, fighting corruption in any way I can. I pray this book will go a long way in motivating others to stand with me for God and country.

I and my five classmates were the last graduating class from dear old Rawls High School. From there, I enrolled at Straughn High School near Andalusia, Alabama. In my opinion, Straughn was the best of Covington County's higher education institutions. Of course, a few folks have differing opinions; my wife would be one of them since she attended a rival school.

Relating a little more about my formative years will help explain how I came to be such a passionate American patriot and so protective of our great country. During my days as a student at Straughn High School several influential people entered my life. Thankfully, all the instructors at my school were very competent and caring teachers. Time and space will not allow me to elaborate on all of them. This book is not about me, but about fixing America. I only digress into my early life to give the reader a glimpse into where such passionate patriotism has its genesis. I must mention at this point my esteemed high school coach. Coach Doyle Kinsaul taught History, and his charming wife Jackie taught English. I shall forever be appreciative to her for exposing me to the many great literary authors and their works. I feel indebted to Coach Kinsaul for teaching me the fine points of basketball and how to be a team player. Dedicated men like Coach Kinsaul care more about making men out of boys than winning games. Men like him make this country great. Don't misunderstand me. He did want us to be winners, and win we did, most of the time. More importantly, he wanted us to be winners in life as well as on the hardwood basketball floor. Coach Kinsaul was my mentor and continues to be one of my heroes. (Coach, if you ever read this, you can be confident that I attribute any degree of success that I may have attained as an educator and coach to you and your firm, but caring guidance and mentorship.)

Networking, I am told, is a very vital and essential ingredient to success these days. I reckon I don't disagree because the next important man responsible for who I am today, was out "networking" when he met me. (Not that I am somebody.) I consider myself to be a nobody, bold enough to tell everybody about somebody who can save anybody. I get that boldness from one of the most dedicated men of God I have ever met. I speak of the Reverend Alfred Ikner, an old fashioned Baptist preacher with an old fashioned message. He preached the wonders of God's grace and the matchless love of our Heavenly Father for over fifty years, serving as pastor to more than twenty Southern Baptist churches. When we laid him to rest on a sad day in 2012, the church did not have nearly enough room to seat the hundreds of loving people who came to pay their last respects to a man who had no doubt done for them what he had done for me. He had performed the marriages of many people attending. Others, Reverend Ikner had baptized. Some were there who had heard him preach and whose lives were touched by his message. Many came who only knew him as a neighbor who cared enough to help them through difficult times. I was privileged as one of his sons-in-law to officiate at the graveside service. Being at that place of honor is a story in itself. I will share briefly how that came to be. I was chopping firewood to ward off the November chill of 1968 at that same tenant house where I had hidden the white lightning, when a strange man driving a green Pontiac came tearing down the dusty road. He might have worked for the Lord, but he drove like the devil. The man who got out of the car and introduced himself was a small man, not over five feet eight. However, when he suited up in the armor of God, he was a giant of a man. This day he had come prepared to do battle with his arch enemy, the ruler of darkness. Every piece of armor was in place and two kingdoms were about to clash. A pious paragon of pristine protection seemed to cast a surreal aura around this warrior of the Lord. Hanging in the balance was the eternal fate of the bootlegger's boy. I was only fifteen at the time and had given very little thought to my eternal destiny. I did not realize it at the time, but I was a slave in bondage to the ruler of darkness. This little/big man had come to defeat my captor and set me free. I had never met a preacher in person. I had heard a few on our TV like the Reverend Billy Graham. As far as I knew, only the murderers, thieves, whoremongers, and other hard-core criminals needed Jesus. I was not aware that a bootlegger's boy needed to be washed in the blood. He set about to enlighten me and before I knew it, I was a born again believer. I was now part of His network. I was a child of the King and a member of the Kingdom of Heaven.

I had not attended very many services at Gantt Baptist Church before I realized, to my delight, that this man of God was the father of three very lovely girls. He would later on have a fourth. I am married to the pick of the litter. They were all very charming, you understand, but I married the loveliest one. I had first pick. All's fair in love and war. This did not happen without much ado. Patsy had other suitors, but I was lucky. Rev. Ikner liked me more than he did them. I could tell because he threatened them with a shotgun. He only threatened me with a "butt whupin" if I misbehaved around his daughter. So, for the second time in a month he planted the fear of God in my heart, and I believed he would follow through on his promise. On one occasion he "pertneer" put a whoopin on a wayward, out of order deacon who was threatening the harmony of the congregation. I know he was a true man of God because he later regretted and wholeheartedly repented of his mistake of losing his temper in dealing with that deacon. I know he was a true man of God also because of his strict adherence to the Word. I recall that Jacob had to work seven years for Laban in order to get his permission to marry his daughter Rachel. I guess Rev. Ikner thought he would teach me some more scripture, by letting me work awhile for his daughter Patsy. The First Baptist Church of Gantt, Alabama was in the midst of a building project at the time, and I was right in the middle of it all. I poured concrete, nailed on shingles and performed every other job involved in building the new pastorium. I didn't mind, I figured it was a small price to pay in order to see my sweetheart without fear of bodily harm. On July 23, 1971, the pick of the litter and I were married.

In the years that followed, my wife and I both attended college and received teaching degrees. We were in a number of small schools in Alabama, Georgia, and Florida and met some very wonderful people along the way. I wanted every one of my students and boys that I coached to think of me in the same way I thought of my high school coach. I know I failed in this respect at times through mistakes that rookie coaches make, but I feel confident that I have made a few positive contributions to those entrusted to my care.

The experiences I went through during my teaching career further solidified my patriotism and stoked the fire of passion to one day do more to make an impact for the betterment of the country I love so much. One of my degrees is in biology, so at most of my coaching stops, I was also given the teaching assignments of biology, physical science, and chemistry. Now if you have not been there and done that, you do not know how hard it is to teach those subjects with a laboratory consisting of a dozen test tubes and a few worn out Bunsen burners. In most cases I had to do fund-raisers to raise money to buy lab equipment. I knew there were problems in educational priorities when at one school I was given a budget of $2500 to buy new football equipment and $200 for the science lab. I was grateful for the sports money because I love sports and realize that participating in those activities also builds character and helps in the overall development of young people if it is done in the right manner. I vowed right then to get involved in politics one day and try to get into a position to make things better for education. I was, however, unsuccessful in my one bid for public office, and somehow my ego could not bear the thought of ever losing another election. I do not have the tenacity that Abraham Lincoln and many others possessed which motivated them to try again. This book will be my contribution to try to improve not only education, but other aspects in America that need attention.

At least two houses need attention in America today. One is the White House that sits on top of Capitol Hill, and the other is "our house" the American home. By correcting the problems that emanate from these houses, we will solve a multitude of evils. We have weasels in the hen house and vicious termites gnawing away at the foundations of our democracy. Sadly, blood-sucking parasites are hiding in every nook and cranny. Disease-carrying cockroaches are spreading the plague of socialism throughout our sacred halls of government. These vermin must be eradicated at all cost.

AUTHOR'S NOTE

INTRODUCTION TO PHOTO SECTION

Some readers may question the inclusion of family photos in a book about fixing America's problems. My thinking and that of my editor's is that this collection of photos will help the reader to establish who the author is and to identify with his motivation for writing the book. My personal life values are God, family, and country—in that never-changing order. My sincere desire is for all Americans to acknowledge God, to love and support their families, and to re-affirm the Pledge of Allegiance to the United States of America, support our Constitution and become responsible contributing citizens of our nation.

I challenge all readers as they review my family photos, to think of their own families and realize that we must all act with more common sense if our values, freedoms and opportunities are to be preserved for posterity.

Fletcher English, Covington County's most notorious bootlegger.
Author, Ken English, 5-year old bootlegger's son.

Author, Ken English, 5th grade, Rawls High School.
(1963—the year I hid the moonshine in the outhouse.)

VARSITY BASKETBALL TEAM: STRAUGHN HIGH SCHOOL—1971
Left to Right: Bill Butler, Johnny Bryars, Ricky Bass, Horace Franklin,
Hayward Smith, Dorman Nelson, Ken English, Delbert Blocker.
Coach Doyle Kinsaul

Senior Portrait: Straughn High School: 1971

Here, I am trying hard to score against county rival,
Andalusia High School, January, 1971.

1971 BASEBALL TEAM

Left to right front row—Bill Graham, Zane Tucker, Johnny Bryas, William Blocker, Bill Butler, Gary Kelly, Randy Stewart Left to right back row—Willie Van Walker, Andy Kelly, Audrey Walker, Anthony Ammons, Ken English, Jim Yant, Elbert Cunningham, Lamar Lawson, Coach Doyle Kinsaul

VARSITY BASEBALL TEAM: STRAUGHN HIGH SCHOOL. I
probably had the lowest batting average on the team. I was given a uniform
because the coach needed another warm body to shag fly balls during
batting practice. (I am in the center on the back row)

Wedding day at the First Baptist Church, Gantt, Alabama—July 23, 1971. (Left to right: Rev. Alfred Ikner, Elaine Ikner, (parents of the bride,) Patsy Ikner, Ken English, Lorene English Estes, (my sister,) Fletcher English, (father of the groom.)

My wife, Patsy poses with me at my ordination service. Salem Baptist Church, near Andalusia, Alabama.

Rev. and Mrs. Alfred Ikner. Two wonderful and
caring servants of the Lord.

Coaching days: Coffee Springs High School, 1989. Here I discuss strategy
with soph. wide receiver, Tony Simmons and assistant coach, Mike Moore.
We won this play-off game against Southern Normal, 30-12.

Warren Bowran, (right) head of the Tri-county Football Officials, presents me with the Football Coach of the Year Award—1989.

I was privileged to meet former Governor, George C. Wallace after his presidential campaign. Here, I present him with one of my first sculptures of Coach "Bear" Bryant.

In 1996, I was commissioned by the city of Enterprise, AL. to make a replica of the famous Boll Weevil Monument. Here, I am on a scaffold in downtown Enterprise making the mold for the casting. The Replica was put on display at the Atlanta History Museum during the 1996 Olympics.

In 1986, I was a sales representative for United Surgical Steel Co. In this photo, I am in Hawaii trying to sell some surgical steel to a well-known private investigator.

The English Family during my coaching days At Coffee Springs High School near Enterprise, Alabama. Ken, Patsy, Kyle, Jennifer.

In 1994, we acquired a cattle ranch and named it The Big Oak Ranch. Here, Patsy and I prepare to take Thunder and Blue for a ride to inspect fences.

Inspecting the hay field in preparation for the first hay cutting in 1997.

My son Kyle, and loyal cow-dog Jeb, prepare to round up some calves. (Kyle preferred riding a four-wheeler as opposed to a four-legger.)

I don't know who was more excited about the first foal born on the Big
Oak Ranch, Princess, our cherished Belgian, or me.

I am taking my Belgians, Queen and Princess to the barn after plowing
five acres. (I am brave enough for Roman riding only when the
team is too tired to run away.)

Getting the garden ready for Spring planting on the Big Oak Ranch.

Both my kids were always involved in sports. Here, I pose with Kyle
in his first year of Little League baseball

Exploring the Pea River with my son, Kyle and daughter, Jennifer.

Escorting my daughter, Jennifer, during a high school beauty pageant.

My wife and I always held our breath when our daughter did stunts as Captain of the Troy University Cheerleaders.

It seems that I never could afford to hire ranch hands to share the hard work on the Big Oak Ranch, so I cloned a replica of myself. The clone does very well as a sentry but is useless when it comes to hauling hay or mending fences.

Patsy supervises Davin and Ayden, (our oldest grandsons)
as they take their first ride on "Sparky".

Here, I am in my blacksmith shop forging some metal parts for my carriage.

The finished product, complete with dashboard and radio!

Kyle's last football game at Elba High School. Sister, Jennifer, was there to cheer him on.

Ken, Patsy, and Jennifer attend Kyle's high school graduation ceremony.

Patsy prepares the gazebo at the Big Oak Ranch for
Kyle's wedding reception

My son-in-law, Jason McCoy, and my daughter Jennifer,
pose with my son Kyle and his bride, Kaci, during their wedding
reception at the Big Oak Ranch.

Gathering turnips seems to be an extremely funny experience
for "Pat-Pat" and Grand-son Ayden.

Papa Ken with our first two grandsons: Davin McCoy and Ayden English.

Patsy and I tour D.C. as I search the city for "MORE COMMON SENSE"

CHAPTER I

COMMON SENSE MUST BE REVIVED

In 1776 an unlikely character named Thomas Paine wrote one of the most influential books in the history of America. At the time of his writing, our young country was in turmoil. The average citizen was being taxed beyond his ability to cope. The very survival of many hung perilously in the balance. Voices cried for revolution and a clean break from the mother country. For a revolution to succeed against such a powerful nation as England, every able-bodied man in the colonies would be needed. We could ill afford to have very many of our countrymen remain loyal to the crown. This was, however, the case. Many Americans, in spite of the hardships they were enduring as a direct result of the crown, were hesitant to bear arms against the mother country. A little book called "Common Sense" finally persuaded many colonists to join the revolution. How could one little book be so successful in swaying the masses? To answer this question we must delve into the history of our country a little deeper. First of all, most of the colonists were Godly people. They had left England and other parts of Europe mainly to seek religious freedoms not available in the old country. The president of Argentina asked a statistician on one occasion, "Why is South America, with all its natural advantages: its mines of iron, copper, coal, silver, gold, its rivers, and great waterfalls which rival Niagara—so far behind North America?" The statistician replied, "Well, Mr. President, it could be because South America was settled by the Spanish who came to South America in search of gold while North America was settled by the Pilgrims who went there in search of God." Keep this in mind when I tell you the main thrust and gist of Paine's "Common Sense."

When we investigate the common sense used by Paine to convince those wavering on the fence, we find that he actually used the "scientific method." He merely used a three step approach in his persuasion. First, he identified the problem. Second, he found the source of the problem. Third, he recommended a course of action to eliminate the source of the problem. He simply reasoned that if he could eliminate the source of a problem, he could make the problem go away. Simple? Yes, that's what is so great about common sense. You do not need to activate or employ the totality of your cerebral cortex to solve most problems no matter how threatening and ominous they may seem. Take the bubonic plague for example, one of the worlds' most deadly scourges. Literally thousands of people owe their demise to this dreaded disease when there was a common sense solution. Rocket science was not needed. Once they discovered that the plague was transmitted by fleas, it was a no-brainer to figure out that in order to stop the plague, the source of the fleas had to be found and eliminated. You know the rest of the story—millions of rats were slaughtered in order to destroy the source of the fleas. Many more examples of using common sense in science, medicine and industry to solve challenging problems fill our nation's history. We shall concern ourselves, however, with how Paine used his common sense approach to rid America of her plague of indecision.

Paine reasoned, and rightly so, that the source of most of the colonists' problems was a crown and that crown was on the wrong head. He proceeded to explain that the curse on the colonists was not their being subjected to 'A' king but being subjected to 'any' king. Man has only one king, and He is not Elvis, George I, Edward II, or Henry the VIII. He is Jesus Christ our Lord. Paine then conducted a Sunday school lesson and revealed to them why England had a king in the first place. He took them on a journey to Palestine and reminded them how the nation Israel had obtained their first king. No kings reigned in the early ages of the world; therefore, nations had no wars. According to Paine, the kings' pride and greed threw mankind into confusion and war. We only have to look at Holland and study the history of this country without a king to see that Paine was right. Holland has enjoyed more years of peace than any government in Europe. Paine explained further that the heathen nations who God had told Israel to annihilate introduced the customs of having kings into the world. Nevertheless, the children of Israel wanted to be like them and have a king to provide for them and to go out to battle for them. Mr. Paine appealed to his readers' sense of Biblical morality. He informed them that exalting one man so greatly above the rest cannot be justified on the equal rights of nature nor can it be justified or defended on the authority of scripture. The will of God as declared by Gideon and the prophet Samuel expressly disapproves of government by kings. When Paine declared that serving an ungodly king would constitute idolatry, no wonder many colonists saw the error of their ways. In Paine's words, "The Almighty, ever jealous of His honor, absolutely disapproves of a form of government which so impiously invades the prerogative of heaven."

I think we would all be well-served in being reminded that being subservient to any king or a man like Obama, who thinks he is a king, is nothing short of foolish idolatry. People are too easily impressed and too easily deceived. It was P.T. Barnum who said, "People love to be hoodwinked; they take to it like ducks to water." P.T. ought to know. He made thousands of dollars on one deception alone-"Enter here to see the man-eating chicken," read the sign outside the sideshow tent. After paying their hard earned money, circus goers were treated to the sight of a man dressed in a tuxedo, seated at a table. He was devouring a piece of fried chicken. The Israelites during the days of the Judges were constantly oppressed by the Midianites. This barbaric tribe would swoop down on the helpless Jews and steal their crops and cattle year after year. Gideon, empowered by God, was able to defeat them with a small army. The Jews, even though the victory came through divine intervention, attributed the win to Gideon and suggested making him a king saying, "Rule thou over us, thou and thy son and thy son's son." Not only did they offer him a kingship, they offered an extended contract. They offered perpetual rule to one man and his descendants. Being the wise and Godly man that he was, Gideon replied to them, "I will not rule over you, neither shall my son rule over you." According to Paine, Gideon did not decline the honor, but denied their right to give it.

Amazingly, the Israelites did not give up their quest to be like the heathen nations and obtain for themselves a king. Over a hundred years passed, and they came to Samuel again pleading for a king. Samuel took the petition to God who then told Samuel to try to dissuade them by telling them some of the consequences of having a king. These evil and devastating consequences are enumerated in I Samuel, Chapter 8, verses 10 through 18. I exhort my readers to examine these verses carefully to realize the wrongs Samuel warned Israel about are happening in America today. The king would appoint some of their sons for his chariot, some to be his horsemen, and some to run before his chariots. In Paine's day, Americans were being pressed into military service against their will, to fight battles that were not theirs. Sounds familiar does it not? In verse 12 of I Sam. 8, Samuel tells the children of Israel that their king would shanghai their young men or make them plow in the king's field and work in his shops making implements of war. Of course, those things did happen to the early American colonists and guess what. It is happening again in America today. Think of the thousands of Americans today who work for the U.S. Government making instruments of war. A lot of logic exists in the theory that sometimes our "king" declares war for no other reason than to manipulate the economy and create jobs; thereby securing votes for the next election. Verse 15, I Samuel, Chapter 8 is really interesting. Paine points out that Samuel was showing them in this verse that bribery, corruption, and favoritism are the standing vices of sitting kings. Samuel's words which came directly from God himself fell on deaf ears as the Israelites persisted in their demands for a king.

After quoting scripture after scripture, Paine's common sense began to ring true in the ears of the early colonists. To add icing to the cake and to drive his point home, Paine further showed them that they, as mere mortals, had no power to give away the rights of posterity. They would surely be forfeiting future generations; by serving and being loyal to a king whose descendants would follow him in power. In Paine's words, "Such a course is unwise, unjust, unnatural, and ungodly; and such a pact might in the next succession to the throne, put them under the government of a rogue, a fool, a minor, or all three rolled into one."

Paine completed his discourse on the evils of hereditary succession in kings by pointing out that a minor at any age and an old king worn out with age, might be susceptible to the betrayal of a regency acting under the cover of a king. In both cases the people become prey to every evil agent who has opportunity to tamper successfully with either the infirmity of age or the gullibility of the young.

Some of the fence sitters offered their genetic ties to England as a reason for remaining loyal to the crown. Paine skillfully shot down this point of contention as easily as William Tell put an arrow through the apple on his son's head. "Admitting that we were all of English descent, what does it amount to? Nothing. Britain, being now an open enemy, extinguishes every other name and title; and to say that reconciliation is our duty is truly farcical. The first king of England, of the present line, (William the Conqueror), was a Frenchman, and half the Peers of England are descendants from the same country; wherefore, by the same method of reasoning, England ought to be governed by France."

I cannot leave our examination of Mr. Paine's common sense without relating one more of the valid points he made to his readers. Time has not erased the applicability and relevancy of his words concerning foreign affairs. Many of the colonists wanted to remain loyal to the crown because they felt that America needed the strength of England to preserve them from enemies abroad. Paine jumped on that one like Lee and Stonewall on a Yankee. He first stated the obvious fact that a nation as young as ours had no enemies, other than by association. Paine made it easy for the undecided to give up this line of reasoning by again applying a little common sense. Where are you, Mr. Paine? America needs you and for an absolute certainty, a man named Obama needs you. He needs you like an overboard Titanic passenger needed a lifeboat. My fellow American, I exhort you to ponder these next words of Mr. Paine and attest to their relevancy today, "What have we to do with setting the world at defiance? Our plan is commerce and that well attended to, will secure us the peace and friendship of all Europe; because it is the interest of all Europe to have America a free port. Her trade will always be protected and her barrenness of gold and silver secure her from invaders." Paine revealed that a King did not have much to do to earn his ridiculous salary and did nothing to deserve the worship heaped upon him. It is shameful that the main business of the King of England was his two favorite pastimes—to make war and give away land, which only served to anger and impoverish the people. His final words on the subject of kings were both true then and apply today to some of our leaders. "Of more worth is one honest man to society and in the sight of God than all the crowned ruffians that ever lived."

Like the "Tories" of Colonial America, many Americans are confused and indecisive. We have been indoctrinated with the influenza of inertia and ignorance and told by our leaders that any movement on our part would be insignificant and ineffective. A bug worse than the West Nile virus has bitten Americans on the butt. We stumble around in a brainless fog and drunken stupor. We follow the pied piper of polluted politicians like we cannot think for ourselves. Paine's original injection of common sense into the American blood stream has worn out, been lost, or rendered impotent. We need a booster shot with a sharp hypodermic, injected directly into our brain. If injected into the butt, the vital serum would take too long to get to the point where the cancerous tumor of apathy grows out of control. The "baboons" in Washington D.C. (By the way, it is a fact that, for maybe some good reason, a group of baboons is not called a herd or a pride or a flock, but a "CONGRESS") have brainwashed, bamboozled, ballyhooed, and bull-buttered us long enough. Now is a good time for a rally of not only the Republicans, but of all the redeemed in America. Congress has censored, crossed out, and corrupted our Creator and His Commandments long enough. Wake up, my Fellow Countrymen! Not only are we living in the bountiful land of milk and honey, but, also a large proportion of us are children of the King or at least claim to be at tax time when we list our tithes as deductions. As Americans and children of the Most High, we deserve better. The newly freed Jews left Egypt with such big plans and ambitions to be a free people, but after crossing the Red Sea they wandered in circles for forty years. From Egypt to the Promised Land was only a short distance. Going by foot should have taken only a matter of weeks to get there. What happened? They did not get lost because God led them with a cloud in the daytime and a fire by night. Once again, the problem was a lack of common sense. They were disobedient to the God who defeated their enemies and overcame so many adversities for them. I firmly believe that we are wandering in the wilderness and suffering many unnecessary adversities simply because we have been disobedient to the same God. The cure for the apathy, laziness, and the impoverished predicament in which most Americans find themselves is, once again, a quickly applied poultice of potent common sense. I am convinced that when we return to the solid Rock foundation, God, who made this country possible, will once again act in our favor and restore to us the blessings of life, liberty and the pursuit of happiness.

The Jews were a free people after they crossed the Red Sea. Their slave masters were drowning at the bottom of that body of water, no longer to drive them, no longer to beat them, and no longer to impose their will upon them. Again, I call your attention to the fact that they did not go immediately to the Promised Land. They did not immediately sip the milkshakes and munch on honey toast. Although they were a free people, they still reasoned with a slave mentality. They were not suited for nor did they deserve freedom, living as they were, in their perverted mental state and disobedient heart condition. They were never disowned. God never completely forsook them. They were in no danger of starving to death since God miraculously fed them with manna every day. They even had occasional treats of fresh meat. They never lacked for clothes or shoes. God miraculously saw to it that their shoes had a lifetime guarantee and never wore out. God's care for them was better than the Wal-mart plan of which so many Americans take unfair advantage by returning a slightly used but maybe not defective item to the service department for exchange.

Folks, we are so much like them that the similarities are amazing. Many Americans today are too lazy to work and are happy to lie around on the couch, watch a TV that the government bought for them, eat food the government provided for them, and belly ache about the inadequacies of our republic. Children of these misguided, misinformed, and mistaken Americans are raised to continue the cycle. They are educated on how to get "free money" before they are taught the multiplication tables or how to conjugate a verb. They are very astute and eager students but only listen when Momma and Papa talk about free money and no work. Such people know more about how to bilk the government than Pythagoras knew about triangles. We must re-educate our children to a new way of thinking. They must be taught the work ethics of old. They must learn to rely on their own creativity, initiative, and God given abilities. They must have a new vision of how much better life is when they work for themselves instead of depending on the government. They must see that dependency on any government, be it a monarchy or republic, is just another form of slavery. Obama is lying when he says that we did not create our companies and businesses by sweat, toil, and an honorable work ethic. He is lying when he tells us that everything we have is a result of his good government and stimulus packages. Tell your children that if they will get rid of the "slave mentality," they will once again see God work in mighty ways. Tell your children that our strength lies not in numbers, but in unity. We must learn to love our fellow man regardless of color, creed, or economic status. We must teach our children that they are their brothers' keeper. Yes, my friend, we are wandering in the wilderness just like the Jews of old, and the same thing that fixed their problem can fix ours. Scripture tells us, "if we will acknowledge Him in all our ways, He will direct our paths" (Proverbs 3:6)

At this point, I am advocating a government "makeover" as opposed to a government "takeover." I am optimistic that if we will elect a true man of God to fill the oval office and surround him with a cabinet of Godly advisors like Mike Huckabee, John Hagee, Billy Graham, and many others who would fit the bill, America could be returned to greatness. Only a nation that honors God can receive the blessings of God. Until that happens, we are certainly going to continue to reap the bitter harvest of the bad seeds sown by a selfish and godless government. Folks,the most serious problem facing America today is not "emissions" from autos and industrial plants but "omissions," the most serious of which is our government's omission of God. Review Lincoln's Gettysburg Address; "We here highly resolve, that these dead shall not have died in vain; that this nation, under God, shall have a new birth of freedom, and that the government of the people, by the people, and for the people shall not perish from the earth." If we omit two vital words, **under God,** a government of the people, so described, may be little more than a form of tyranny. When we include these two vital words, we have something radically different and tremendously better. If we can once again be "a nation under God," we will then have a nation that honors God and submits to His righteous rule and will thereby be exalted and blessed. Psalms 33:12 tells us, "Blessed is the nation whose God is the Lord."

Not only have we forgotten God, but we have also banned and forbidden Him. We have dismissed and ignored His truths. We must seek His favor by establishing His truth if America is to return to the glory and beauty of her infancy. As we embrace truth, I would share three things about the truth of God that we must remember. First, The Truth of God is transcendent. God's wisdom is as far above me and all other mortals as Heaven is above the earth. Second, His truth is transported. Truth came to earth by a living person, Jesus Christ. If it had not been so transported, truth would be of no value to creatures on this earth. Finally, God's truth is transforming. Once embraced and accepted, it changes our values and reorients our thinking so that we will no longer believe the lies of Satan, the father of lies, or corrupt politicians who are his emissaries and who perpetuate his lies.

The function of government in regard to the individual is to recognize and defend our inalienable, God given rights of freedom, security, and the opportunity to pursue happiness and success. When the government ceases to do this or fails in its attempts, it is time to make corrections and changes. Not only is our present government failing in this, but it is actually making it harder for the individual to survive. Man is being dehumanized by our "dog-eat-dog" society. While at the same time, our welfare-minded government devitalizes him, and our high tech, mechanized and industrialized work environment minimizes man.

I am reminded about a very singular and interesting event that occurred in Philadelphia as our founding fathers were hammering out our new constitution. After all the mighty men brave enough to sign that document, knowing that they might be signing their very lives away, had put the quill back into the inkpot, Benjamin Franklin alluded to the rays of light striking the top of the chair in which General George Washington was sitting. He then asked the general and all the esteemed gentlemen gathered there, "Are the rays of light from a rising or setting sun?" Washington asked Franklin what he thought, and the great man of science and philosophy who knew a little bit about nature's rays of energy, replied, "It is a Rising Sun." We need to ask that same question about the light that illuminated Obama's face during a church service which prompted some members of the clergy and few choir members to marvel and chant, "This must surely be a sign that he is the chosen one." My comment on their response is "Hogwash, bull-butter, and what have you fellows been smoking?" Our man Obama might have been chosen, but he was not chosen by God. When God picks a man, He picks a winner. He looks at the heart and not the oratory. Israel chose the wicked and ungodly Saul for king. God never did. He chose the young man David, a man after God's own heart. No, I'm afraid that if God were captain and Obama was among the many to be chosen for the dodge ball game at recess, he would be the last little nerd to be picked. No, wait! Maybe Satan might recognize his talent at dodging the real issues, dodging the truth, and dodging his responsibilities, and pick him first for his team.

Unfortunately my Friends, the sun is not rising in America today. Darkness is descending upon us. We live in troubled times, desperate times! Unless global solutions are found for global problems, our glorious empire will falter and crumble just like the Roman Empire. The solutions to so many of our problems require nothing more than all of us rising up with one voice of common sense and demanding that our leaders look out for the interests of America. It has been said, "In order for evil to prevail, all that is required is for good men to do nothing." Herbert Hoover said "Our greatest danger is suicide by compliance with evil." We are at that point now. We can no longer sit back and do nothing. Each of us must do his part. Sadly, too many of our American people will forego the rigorous exercise required for any critical thinking. So many people have let the politicians think for them for so long that if their common sense produced a creative thought, I fear that it would die of loneliness. If we don't awaken out of our incoherent stupor and learn to involve ourselves in the process of our government, we shall surely reap the unpleasant and inevitable fruits of laziness and apathy that we have sown. The rotting carcass of a corrupt civilization has only the terrible approach of the vultures of judgment ahead. I know this sounds like a dismal doomsday theory, but it is true. We must return to common sense. We must not let the idea of a personal God, who cares about His creatures and governs in the affairs of men, die in America. I cannot help but think of a joke that circulated in the Baptist churches for years. A hitchhiker was picked up by a fast-driving Baptist minister who drove like Obama is driving this country, recklessly and with very little regard for the rules of the road. Visibly shaken and scared by a few near collisions and some horn blowing by other drivers, the hitchhiker requested that the minister stop at the next service station and let him off. "Don't worry," said the preacher, "God is riding with us." To which the hitchhiker responded, "Well, you had better let me drive. You are going to kill both of us." I sincerely feel that as long as we let an ungodly man sit in the oval office the welfare of God and the nation will never be safe. What a wonderful nation we would be if all of our presidents would have the convictions that Abraham Lincoln had! Lincoln's well-worn Bible lies in the Lincoln Museum today as a silent testimony that he was no doubt a true Christian. Listen to him on the way to his first inauguration. "I go to assume a task more difficult than that which has devolved upon any other man since the days of Washington. He never would have succeeded but for the aid of Divine Providence, upon which he at all times relied. I feel that I cannot succeed without the same divine blessing which sustained him, and on the same Almighty Being, I place my reliance for support. And I hope you my friends, will all pray that I may receive the divine assistance without which I cannot succeed, but with which success is certain."

I realize that we cannot live in the past, but we can look to the past. We can study our former leaders and follow their common sense course of action. Surely we can see that if a logical, common sense approach to the problems of government worked for them, it should work for us today. You may read in your history book how George Washington found rest and relief in prayer during the trying times he and his men passed through at Valley Forge. With all the cares and anxieties of that time upon him, Washington would often rely on prayer. One day a farmer approaching Washington's camp heard an earnest voice. On coming nearer, he saw George Washington on his knees, his cheeks wet with tears, praying to God. The farmer returned home and said to his wife, "General Washington will succeed! The Americans will secure their independence!" "What makes you think so, Isaac?" asked his wife. The farmer replied, "I heard him pray, Hanna; out in the woods today, and the Lord will surely hear his prayer. He will, Hannah; thee may rest assured. He will." Join me, Fellow Americans, in praying the same prayer that a little eight year old boy prayed in Sunday school after being told that daddies will sometimes allow them to take the wheel of the car, but will always place their hands over their little ones to be sure there will be no mistake, "Dear Lord, will you please put your hands over the hands of our president so he will know how to turn the wheel for our country."

A most obvious fact is evident in America today; common sense just isn't as abundant as it used to be. I like to think of common sense as a sixth sense, given to us by our Creator to keep us from misusing the other five senses. It is time for all Americans to start using this God-given gift and stop letting misguided elected officials do our thinking for us.

CHAPTER II

GOD MUST BE RECOGNIZED AND RE-INSTATED

Jeremiah Wright wants God to "Damn America," I want God to "Bless" America. Which one of us gets his wish is up to "we the people." I am confident that God will bless America and bless us richly if we will meet the requirements of those blessings. The blessings of God have seemingly been in short supply in America lately and the reason might just be the way we have forgotten, ignored, and insulted God. Ronald Reagan said, "If ever we forget that we are "one nation under God," then we will be a nation gone under." God might decide to let us hit "rock bottom" in America, so that we will re-discover that He is the "ROCK AT THE BOTTOM".

Knowing the many blessings that God has bestowed on America and realizing how miraculously He has preserved this nation, I ask, "How have we forgotten God?" His footprints are unmistakable and indelible in the fertile soil of our history. Even before the Declaration of Independence or the Constitution, the Mayflower Compact dedicated both the pilgrims on board and the unexplored country to God.

In order to justify a statement about re-instating God in America, I must first establish the fact that God was indeed involved in the founding of America and the constitution by which we are supposed to be governed. To ascertain if God was part of the architecture of the constitution of America, we must thoroughly examine the architects who sat in Independence Hall in Philadelphia in 1787, for surely every house or institution bears the birthmarks of its builders. This was never more certain or evident than in the construction of our constitution.

This document overflows and exudes the very heart and soul of those great men who penned its noble words and unless I am grossly mistaken, the hearts and souls of most of these great men were attuned to the one true God.

If you will dust off your history book and read again the early progression of this constitutional convention, you will see how unlikely it would be that anything of great consequence could be accomplished. There were a multitude of problems that had to be, and were overcome in order for the great task to be completed. First, consider that every man who sat in this assembly had come at his own expense—these men were not highly paid as their modern-day counterparts are. At first only seven of the thirteen states had sent representatives. Before the job was completed, twelve states were finally represented. Second, the mindset and thinking of this group was very diverse. Some wanted a strong central government with almost no control given to the states. Others, remembering the powerful monarchy from whence they came, did not ever want to be subjected to such unbridled power again, and so argued for states' rights. Third, the issue of slavery presented a major problem that had to be dealt with. In fact, some representatives from the South proclaimed that they would never vote to ratify the Constitution if there were any hint of antislavery wording in the Constitution. Fourth, but certainly not last, was the issue of how to deal with the disparity of population among the states. It seemed at times that these and other issues would present insurmountable obstacles that could not be overcome.

According to John Eidsmoe, in his book *Christianity and the Constitution,* George Washington, the presiding convention chairman, was so thoroughly discouraged that he wrote to a friend saying, "I doubt that this convention will ever agree on a new plan of government."

If there is any doubt that God was involved in the laying of our constitutional foundation, the words of Benjamin Franklin, the oldest representative present, should forever establish the fact that God was indeed an integral and vital part of the establishment of our government. Here is a small portion of that speech; "The small progress we have made after four or five weeks is melancholy proof of the imperfection of Human Understanding. We need the Father of lights to illuminate our understanding." Franklin reminded his fellow delegates of how they had prayed regularly to God during the War for Independence in that very hall. "Our prayers were heard and answered." Franklin continued, "Have we forgotten that powerful friend? Or do we imagine that we no longer need His assistance? I have lived, Sir, a long time, and the longer I live, the more convincing proofs I see of this truth—that God governs in the affairs of men. And if a sparrow cannot fall to the ground without His notice, is it probable that an empire can rise without His aid? We have been assured, Sir, in the sacred writings, that 'except the Lord build the House they labor in vain that build it.' I firmly believe this; and I also believe that without His concurring aid we shall succeed in this political building, no better than the builders of Babel." After the speech Franklin recommended daily prayers to be led by various Philadelphia clergymen.

Several questions emerge at this point: Did the rest of the delegates agree with Franklin in his admission of the need for Divine intervention in the construction of our constitution? Did they, in fact, passionately plea for God's wisdom to be showered upon them or did they merely tolerate the prayers of the ministers who offered the prayers? Did God grace Independence Hall with his Divine presence? Did He bring unity and peace out of the discord and hostility that pervaded the air in the early days of the constitutional convention? Is God's indelible mark and input unquestionable as we examine the words of this magnificent document?

I am convinced that the answers to these questions are easily answered if we examine the backgrounds and core beliefs of these men who drafted the world's most significant government document. As John Eidsmoe so beautifully stated: "these men may have come to America empty-handed, but they did not come empty-headed." Indeed, they all brought remnants of their heritage and culture with them. These intelligent and pious men knew that they did not have to start from scratch in forming a new government. They realized that there already existed many sound and common-sense ideas that had proven over time to work very well in the governing of a sinful society. Our founding fathers who framed the Constitution were very intelligent, well-educated, and sensible men who incorporated the best ideas of the old country into our new form of government.

So, what did the majority of the framers of the Constitution believe? Whose ideas did they subscribe to? What books did they read? Who was the greatest influence on their way of thinking? The answers to these and other important questions are all tucked away in the annals of our history. Because so many of our founding fathers came from Calvinistic backgrounds, I can accurately state that John Calvin was the father of our constitution.

As Calvinists-influenced believers, what would our founding fathers have believed? Among other things they would have believed in the total depravity of human nature, the priesthood of all believers due to the sacrifice of Jesus Christ on the cross, God's law as revealed in the Bible is always relevant to modern society, covenant theology, and that civil government is ordained by God with only limited authority.

Many people today are under the false assumption that many of our founding fathers were Deists. What do Deists believe? They believe that God created the universe and established physical laws which would regulate a world from which He had forever withdrawn. Nicolaus of Oresmes describes a Deist in terms of a watchmaker who creates a watch, winds it up, and leaves it—never to adjust or intervene again. According to my research, only three of the fifty-five delegates to the 1787 constitutional convention were listed as Deists. Ben Franklin was one of the three listed as a Deist. However, his statement about God and his request for prayer to invoke the direct intervention of God in helping to construct the Constitution, assures me beyond any shadow of doubt, that Ben Franklin was not a Deist in his adult life.

Ninety-five percent of the 55 delegates attending the Constitutional Convention in 1787 were members of Christian churches ranging from Episcopalian to Methodist. Most churches in colonial America required that all members swear to their belief in the Bible as God's revelation and to pledge their faith in Jesus Christ.

Professor Donald S. Lutz did extensive research with one goal in mind—to determine which European Thinkers influenced the framers of our constitution and to what extent. Lutz discovered that the Bible was the source most often cited by our founding fathers. Outside the Bible, there were many great thinkers who had significant impact on the men who laid the foundation document of America. Leading the list of great minds who influenced the writers of our constitution were; Baron Charles Montesquieu, Sir William Blackstone, and John Locke. What do all these men have in common? They were Christians who believed that all law originates from God.

Knowing how much of our constitution has its origin in the Bible and realizing that it was penned by devout men of God, it is most difficult for me to understand how far away from God and our Christian heritage that America has moved.

When did we decide that we no longer need God? Why did we vote him out of our schools? When did we say that His commandments could no longer be displayed in court rooms? When we exploded the first atomic bombs in Japan, did we get the notion that we had the power of God and no longer needed Him? Did we decide to retire Him as CEO of our nation when our astronauts first walked on the lunar surface in 1969? In our infinite wisdom, did we reason that having satellites in space to pinpoint coordinates on earth, eliminated our need for God to show us where we are in the universe? Maybe we abandoned God when our scientists cracked the DNA code and charted the human genome. Compared with God's omnipotent power the atomic bombs are but firecrackers. He put on a little fireworks display Himself many eons ago. Unbelievers call it the "Big Bang"...and so it was. Creation was not a big deal with God! He whispered, "Bang," and the foundations of the universe appeared. God said, "Let there be light, and there was light" (Gen. 1:3); that sounds like a "Big Bang" to me.

The moon landing was big news in 1969. Walter Kronkite had a field day with that one. The U.S. would forever have bragging rights in the space race with the Ruskies. Landing on the moon was indeed a giant leap for mankind, but God holds the moon in His hand like a kid holds a marble. All of our GPS systems would go haywire, and work about as well as two tin cans and a string, if God decided on a whim to have a little fun and move the earth just a few degrees right or left, or tilt it a few degrees off the standard twenty three and one half degrees. We all have reason to be excited and optimistic about DNA code being deciphered. Knowing the human genome will open the doors for many cures of lethal and debilitating diseases. However, God is probably smiling about how long it took us to get this far when it only took him a nano-second to draw up the genetic blueprint of every species of plants and animals on the planet.

America, we had better remember our roots. We must remember God made us from the dust of the ground. We are not the result of spontaneous generation. We are not an accident of the cosmos. Intelligent life (in our case, semi-intelligent) does not spring forth out of nothing on its own. I have never tried this, but I am convinced that if I took a pocket watch, dismantled it piece by piece without losing a single gear or spring, put all the parts into a paint can, sealed the top and shook the can for one hundred years; I would never get a working watch again. Yet our Atheist friends would have us believe this. Our bodies are infinitely more complicated than a pocket watch with infinitely more parts. An intelligent creator lies behind the universe and the life forms that populate it. That creator is God Almighty, reigning from His throne. He is the Sovereign Lord of all. We must acknowledge Him and re-instate Him to His rightful place of honor in this country.

In the movie "City Slickers", one of the tenderfoots asks a seasoned, wrinkled old cowboy named Curly, "What is the secret of life?" Curly would never answer the question orally but would always hold up the index finger of his right hand to answer the inquiry. This was baffling to the greenhorn cowboys who had signed up for the cattle drive to get away from city life to seek a new meaning and purpose for their lives. Near the end of movie they discovered what the one finger held up meant. They were to have one single purpose, or one main focus in life. They must not be distracted and sidetracked. He was somehow telling them that their lives were confused and complicated because they had allowed too many insignificant matters to overshadow the main goal.

We have allowed the same thing to happen all across this great land of ours. In our quest for more and more things, in our quest for significance, and in our desire to "be somebody", we have pushed God out of our lives. America has forgotten what our founding fathers said about God. Our nation has minimized His role in the birth and establishment of our young republic. We have listened to a few atheists and evolutionists and let a very small minority of people dictate what we can or cannot do with the God of the universe.

Barry Switzer, former head football coach of the Oklahoma Sooners was trying to get into the house of a high priority recruit in Texas named Andre Johnson. Ms. Johnson, the boy's mother, had already ordered an assistant coach off the property. Ms. Johnson was barring the door with a scowl on her face when Barry went to try again. "I know you Barry Switzer", chirped Ms. Johnson, "I know all about that gang of outlaws you call football players up in Oklahoma, Well, ya'll ain't gettin my son, so go on outta heah." While she was scolding him, his nose picked up a familiar smell coming from her kitchen…a smell that took Barry back to his childhood. "Is that cracklin bread I smell?" "By golly, it is….isn't it Ms. Johnson?" She looked at Barry suspiciously and quizzed, "What would you know about cracklin bread?" It so happens that Irma Reynolds, Barry's black grandmother, made it for him when he was growing up. (For those of you who don't know—a "cracklin" is a deep fried pig skin, not to be confused with a "chitlin.") Barry continued his discussion of cracklin bread, "It's been years since I've had a piece of cracklin bread. I don't know why you hate me, I've never done you or your son any harm. I respect your right to throw me off your property, but you couldn't hate me so much that you would deny me a piece of that bread. Have you got any buttermilk?" She invited him in, and he ate two pieces and asked for some to go. After seeing how much he enjoyed the bread, she invited him to sit down in the living room to chat. Pretty soon, as it always does when a coach is on a recruiting mission, the subject of football came up. Coach Switzer told the whole Johnson family enthusiastically how he expected that Andre would start his first year in the SECONDARY. "Wait a minute coach," Ms. Johnson said, "I don't want my boy playing in no SECONDARY." "If I let Andre go to Oklahoma, I expect him to play in the FIRSTDARY."

Fellow Americans, let me assure you of one indisputable fact. God is not going to "play in America's SECONDARY!" He will not play "second fiddle" in any orchestra. He will not take a back seat. Why, He won't even ride "shotgun." He must be in the driver's seat. For too long we have inscribed His name on our coins but refused to embed Him in our hearts. We cannot be a Christian nation if God is not the boss and always playing in the "FIRSTDARY."

My dream for America closely resembles Dr. Martin Luther King's American dream. I envision a president walking out on the White House balcony on his inauguration day and proclaiming, "As for me and my house we will serve the Lord." (Mike Huckabee would have said those words if we had given him the Oval Office. Mike, if you read this, there are many of us here in Alabama that want you to try again.) Whether he is a democrat or republican won't matter. What he says about the economy won't matter. What he says about welfare and a thousand other issues won't matter, because he would have taken care of the most important matter of business. All critical and urgent issues will be handled in a manner that will serve the best interest of the people and glorify God. Because the main thing will have already been established, if a true man of God with just a smattering of common sense and a good background in governance or business leadership can ever gain control of the Oval Office, America can't lose. Such a "Dream President" would have to surround himself with a cabinet of other well-qualified, Godly patriots who want nothing but the best for America. No president would be able to meet the challenges of this position if he selected Barney Fife, Gilligan, Colonel Schulz, Goober Pyle, Jethro Bodine, Roscoe P. Coldtrain, and Earnest T. Bass as members of his staff. (Don't laugh too hard at this great comedic cabinet because it has not been very long ago that a president did surround himself with such funny and unqualified advisors.) All great football dynasties had two things in common: First, they all had great men at the top who knew how to use the talents and abilities of a trusted staff with maximum efficiency. Second, they all had a staff of well-qualified loyal men who knew how to be followers and to work together as a team. We could say the same thing about great businesses. The secret is the man at the top, who looks above himself for ultimate counsel and advice.

The last verse in the book of Judges describes not only the situation of the nation of Israel at that time but the situation in America today (Judges 21:25). "In those days, there was no king in Israel; every man did what was right in his own eyes." Allow me to make this distinction. In the case of Israel, not all of the evil was caused by lack of a king; later under some of the kings of Israel, conditions were no better. In the case of America, all of the evil we are seeing results from a denial of God, a disobedience to God, an ignorance of God, and a failure to let Him be Lord of our lives. When God is dethroned, any nation will see an escalation in crime, civil unrest, contextual morality, situation ethics, a disrespect for the rights of others, and anarchy.

Today America must make a decision- a decision just like the one that Joshua, the leader of the Israelites challenged them to make in Joshua 24:15, "...Choose you this day who ye will serve." Americans have had to make some hard decisions in the past. Patrick Henry, a red-headed colonist from Virginia, rose to his feet in an old church in Richmond with a challenge similar to the one Joshua had made, "I know not what course others may take, but give me liberty, or give me death." America's army was small and untrained in the art of war. Having no navy to speak of and no money to fund a war of such magnitude, the early colonists faced a hard choice. To follow Patrick Henry and the other leaders of the revolution, a man had to risk it all. He had to face the possibility of losing his home, his land, and his very life. The Israelites had to make a tough choice as well. They could stay home in the safety of their tents and try to live in peaceful coexistence with the fierce and ungodly enemies that God had told them to drive out, or they could follow Joshua into a battle risking their lives. The choice should not have been hard for the Jews because God had promised them complete victory over these heathen nations. They had already witnessed the miraculous power of God displayed in earlier victories like the easy conquest of Jericho.

America faces the same situation today that Israel faced. The Israelites were in the Promised Land, but they had not eradicated the 31 heathen tribes that occupied the land. They were trying to live in peaceful coexistence, which is a peace without victory. It could not be done then, and it cannot be done today. Douglas MacArthur let us know in no uncertain terms that, "There is no substitute for victory." We today cannot for long peacefully exist with communism, ungodliness, and corruption

We must make, in my opinion, an easy choice, a no-brainer. Ours is not a choice between Scylla or Charybdis, not a choice between Hell and a hot place, not a choice between a rock and a hard place. In other words, it is not a choice between the lesser of two evils. We are deciding between light and darkness, food or famine, war or peace or Heaven or Hell. Our choice comes down to a choice between God, or no God. In my opinion, the common sense option is the former. With the former choice, we have two possibilities; either we win it all if we are right about God, or we lose it all if we are wrong. With the latter choice of **no God** there is only one possibility, and that is to **lose.**

Let me put the choice in one other way and then you decide with common sense which we should choose to guide America. We can either navigate through the uncertain future using the God-created stars which are real and eternal in the heavens, or we can plot our course with St. Elmo's Fire as our beacon in the night. With the former, we shall sail safely into security and sweetness; with the latter we shall surely grind our keel upon the shoals before the night is done. The night is dark; the journey is long. The Philistines and Midianites still stand in our way. We are here in the present-day Promised Land with milk and honey flowing all around us but we can't partake of the spoils of victory until we win the victory. We will have no victory until God is exalted to His rightful place. We can honor God and let Him and His principles guide this nation and be assured of His blessings, or we can continue to live "as those who have no king" and wallow in the pig pen of iniquity, in which case we forfeit God's blessings on us as a nation.

The book of Judges informs us that the Israelites suffered immensely when they left God out of their lives and did what seemed right in their own eyes. I call your attention to the first verse of the Book of Ruth which follows Judges in the Bible. According to Ruth, chapter 1, verse 1; "There was a famine in the land." This is always the case. Famine follows folly. It is also true that feasting follows faithfulness. There is a famine in America today—and it is caused by the same neglect of God that caused the famine in the Book of Ruth.

Our own president leads the way in doing what he thinks is right in his own eyes with a blatant disregard for both the American constitution and God's word. Millions of Americans are following this Hitler-like man who thinks he is a supreme ruler who must answer to no one. A few, like Truett Cathy, founder of Chic-Fil-A, and David

Green, founder of Hobby Lobby are fighting back against the ungodly directives of our misguided leader. In order to put America back on the Godly foundation upon which it was established, we must do likewise. I encourage all of my readers to join me as we rally around a new slogan: "Give us back the freedoms you are taking and have taken from us, or we will have another revolution."

CHAPTER III

THE HOME MUST BE REVIVED AND RE-ESTABLISHED

Many crises face America today; the failing economy, unemployment, illegal immigration, wars, terrorism and the abundance of corruption in positions of leadership. However, an even greater challenge, of which very few people are aware, is threatening our very existence as a nation. The American family is on the endangered species list. If "we the people" do not take steps to strengthen the American home, it will go the way of the great bison and sperm whales. The family unit is deteriorating fast enough on its own without the help of Obama and other liberals trying to establish homosexual marriages as the norm. When we support gay marriage and abortion we are destroying the Biblical idea of a home. The modern movement to deny sexual differences and God-assigned roles is a tool of Satan with one design in mind—destruction of the Christian home. To raze a building quickly, simply plant a charge of dynamite at a strategic point in the foundation. When the foundation crumbles, the building comes down. The Psalmist says in Chapter 11 and Verse 3, "If the foundations be destroyed, what can the righteous do?" and Paul reminds us in I Corinthians, chapter 3, verse 11; "For other foundation can no man lay, than that is laid, which is Jesus Christ." Satan would like to destroy America. The socialists would like to destroy America. They know that the quickest and easiest way to do that is to attack the foundation. That foundation is the home. Likewise, if we would like to preserve our country, we must re-establish and strengthen the homes in America. If the homes in America are restored to the Biblical model and function as God designed them, and if the

Christian churches would work as Christ commanded, many of our government programs would not be necessary. Everywhere we look in America today, we see turmoil, confusion, and political, social, racial, economic, and religious division. Too many people find that they are alienated from God, separated from their neighbor, and sometimes at war with themselves. We need unity and bridges, not walls. Fixing the American home will go a long way toward promoting unity and erasing the social and economic problems that plague our country.

What America needs today more than a tax cut, an oil pipeline, or another airline is to re-establish the direct line of communication to God that we had when homes were the backbone of our country. Several common sense things can be done to restore the home to the standards that are outlined in the Bible.

First of all, establishing a family altar can mightily strengthen the home. To do this successfully, we may have to make some changes. If it is true that "a man's home is his castle," we may have to roll up the drawbridge for a little while to ensure privacy. We may have to turn cell phones off. We may have to hang a sign on the door that reads, "We shoot every third salesman; the second one just left." We may have to sabotage some video games and i-Pods. This done, on a daily basis will give every member of the family strength to meet and deal with the discouragements, disappointments, unexpected adversities, and plans that often go awry. Even a short time spent in this manner will give us an abiding comfort all day long that the God who said, "He would never leave or forsake you," will indeed be by our side. We cannot face each day as a conquistador of Christ unless we first put on His armor, and this will only come through a study of His Word. Having a daily devotion will sweeten home life and enrich home relationships as nothing else can.

Speaking of family relationships, we need to be short on memory and long on forgiveness. Lines of communication must be kept open. Daily devotions, prayer, and Bible study, will ensure that this happens. We will know how effective family devotions are when we see that since we started the family altar, the only scraps we have, are the ones we rake off the dining table. I am reminded of a married couple that was celebrating their 60th wedding anniversary. At the party everybody wanted to know how they managed to stay married so long in this day and age. The husband responded "When we were first married, we came to an agreement. I would make all the major decisions, and my wife would make all the minor decisions. And in 60 years of marriage, we have never had to make a major decision." Surely family devotions not only help in making all decisions, major or minor, but they will help solve all the misunderstandings and relieve most all the frictions that sometimes intrude into the sacred palace of the home.

Next, Parents are obligated to prepare their children for the outside world. No better training and preparation exists than God's instruction manual studied every day. I know as parents we are often tempted to follow Mark Twain's advice on child rearing, "When a kid turns thirteen, stick him in a barrel, nail the lid on the top, and feed him through the knot hole. When he turns sixteen, plug up the knot hole." I think, as always, the Bible has a better idea, "Train up a child in the way that he should go, and when he is old he will not depart from it."(Prov. 22:6) Parents, please remember, in order to obey this advice, both parents and child must spend some quality time at home. Even a family altar won't work if the family is on the three shift schedule: the father on the night shift, the mother on the day shift, and the children having to shift for themselves. This is Biblical truth and does not need any validation from any other source. However, statistics gathered by the Center on Addiction and Substance Abuse at Columbia University confirm that teens who do not eat dinner on a regular basis with their families, as opposed to those who do, are twice as likely to use tobacco and marijuana. They are one and a half times more likely to drink alcohol and more likely to have average or below average grades in school. Look no further than the Waltons for further verification of this; they all got good marks in school, even Jim Bob.

The home should be such a warm, loving, and peaceful place that children would not be inclined to seek their happiness, fulfillment, and love elsewhere. The constitution does not guarantee us happiness but the freedom to pursue happiness. Family devotions will create that freedom where happiness and contentment are more easily found. Children must be taught what a wise old alley cat taught a young kitten on one occasion when the young kitten was observed chasing its tail round and round. The old cat asked, "Why in the world are you chasing your tail like that?" The kitten replied, "I have just graduated from cat philosophy school, and I learned that happiness for a cat is in our tails; so I intend to catch it and hang on to it. Then, I will be perpetually happy." The wise old cat stated, "Well, I never went to cat philosophy school, but I too know that happiness is found in our tail, but I have discovered one thing; When I go forward, forgetting about myself and try to help others, I look back and my tail follows me wherever I go." I am convinced that regular and consistent Bible study will give our children the happiness, confidence, wisdom, and faith to cope with whatever life throws at them. They will not waste time in vain and senseless pursuits.

A lot of families have gotten far away from God. A family altar is the last thing on their minds. A lot of fathers have found the truth in an old Japanese proverb that says, "It's easier to rule a kingdom than to rule a household." That is even truer when the father exhibits a case of the blind leading the blind. The father, as the head of the house, must make sure that he is qualified to lead by studying God's word faithfully and consistently. Unfortunately, one in three children in America lives in a single parent family. The results of being in a single parent home are shocking as told by the National Fatherhood Initiative. Kids in such predicaments have much higher rates of delinquency, alcohol, and drug abuse. They are five times more likely to live at the poverty level, are twice as likely to quit school, and girls from such homes are twice as likely to become teen-aged mothers. According to Mike Huckabee, in his book Simple Government, "Absentee fathers added more than $300 billion to the national deficit in 2010 because of welfare payments. Many of these men were responsible for two or more single parent homes." He goes on to remind us that Russia in 1917 had this same problem and it was deliberately created by the communist government. Guess what, My Friend? The government in America is headed toward this same terrible predicament. If we do not fix the American home soon, we will be exactly where Russia was with families being dependent on the government.

The family dinner table must be brought back. The family altar must be re-instated. Jacob's life was all in a mess. He was disoriented, disillusioned, and distraught. God told him to go back to where he had lost his sense of God and rebuild the family altar at Bethel. Only in this manner could his home and our homes be restored to Godliness. We must all return to Bethel and kindle again a fire of sacrifice and devotion to a God who loves us.

Another thing that must take place to strengthen the home is a cleansing. My mother must have believed that "cleanliness was next to Godliness." She ran a spic and span ship. Not only was she obsessive with every day sweeping, dusting, and making the beds; but once a year she held a major spring cleaning. On this day, all the bedclothes were stripped off the beds, and the mattresses had to be lugged outside so they could "sun." The furniture was moved out of the way, and the floors throughout the house were scrubbed down with lye and Clorox water, using a cornhusk mop or scrubber. I dreaded those days, but I never tried to get out of them by "calling in sick." I learned the hard way that if I did that, she would clean me out with a dose of castor oil. I really appreciate how hard my momma worked to keep that old house as nice and comfortable as possible.

More important than a physically clean house is a spiritually clean house. Certain things and attitudes must be kept out of a Christian home. The Bible records a story of a man in ancient Israel who found out that bringing accursed objects into the home can not only cost him his spiritual victory but cost him his family and his life. After wandering around in the blistering desert for forty years the Children of Israel finally arrived at the Promised Land. God handed them a "hit list of thirty one heathen tribes in Canaan which had to be severely dealt with, and completely eradicated. Jericho was the first city on that list. God's instructions were clear, "And you, by all means, abstain from the accursed things lest you become accursed when you take of the accursed things, and make the camp of Israel a curse and trouble it. But all the silver and gold and vessels of bronze and iron are consecrated to the Lord; they shall come into the treasury of the Lord." (Joshua 6:18, 19)

To note the time that all this occurred is very interesting. The conquest took place on the Jewish calendar between the Feasts of Passover and the Feast of First Fruits. This special time of the year was a time that honored God's blessings on the land. The first ripened fruit of the harvest was to be separated from the rest of the crop and given to God, thus allowing all the remainder of the harvest to be blest of God. This is how God's tithe works: the first fruits of everything, crops, cattle, and income belong to the Lord. If we are greedy and selfish as some Christians have always been, and a large majority is today, we will act like the U.S. Government and "withhold" God's tithe. If they are withheld, not only are they cursed but the act of disobedience brings a curse just as it brought a curse on the entire camp of Israel.

Achan, a member of the tribe of Judah, confiscated some gold and a fine Babylonian garment during the conquest of Jericho and hid it in his tent. What made this a curse was the fact that since this was the first city to be conquered, God had designated all the spoils taken from this first battle as "first fruits" or tithes and had expressly forbidden any soldiers to claim any spoils for personal use. I am sure Achan justified his actions by saying, "I'm doing this for my family. We have been destitute long enough. After all, 'to the victor go the spoils.'" For a short time he thought he had gotten away with his crime. However, his sin would find him out. The second battle in the conquest of Canaan involved the taking of a small city called Ai. This was supposed to be an easy win, like Alabama playing Kent State or some other weak team. Well, on this occasion Kent State beat Alabama. David beat Goliath. Ai was the winner. Israel suffered a humiliating defeat at the hands of a much weaker opponent.

Joshua teaches us a couple of lessons here. The first is a lesson in overconfidence. In this battle he underestimated his opponent and sent his second string to the battle. The Bible tells us the whole story in Joshua Chapter 7. Ai, with a much smaller force, chased 3,000 Israelites out of their city, and like Old Hickory did the British in the 1814 Battle of New Orleans, they chased the Jews through the briars and brambles where a rabbit couldn't go. The second lesson is never to expect a victory in any of life's arenas if we have been disobedient to God.

Only after the accursed treasures were taken out of Achan's tent and put in God's treasury was Israel able to win another victory. Before God will bless nine tenths of our income and make it sufficient, we first have to give Him the first fruits or the first tenth. Listen friend, God doesn't play. They brought Achan and his wife and his children out to the valley of Achor, stoned them to death, and burned the corpses.

What does all this have to do with fixing America? As goes the home, so go the church and the nation. Nothing has changed. God's rules have not changed. If we want His blessings on our homes, our churches, and on our nation, we must be obedient to His word. All this starts with the home. The entire nation was denied a victory because of the sin of one man. How can God bless America with thousands of disobedient Achans out there having the "every man for himself attitude"? We must consider how our actions will affect our relationship with God; how our sins will affect those we love; and how our transgressions will affect our neighbors and our nation. We must not bring accursed things into the home. Today, this includes alcohol, drugs, pornography, or idols of any kind. We cannot bring some things into the home and expect them not to cause hardship or retribution.

I must tell the true story here of my uncle Vernon Waldon. He was two atoms short of a molecule on his best days. When he was drunk, he was an ion. In the early 1960s when most of his neighbors were farming with tractors, he was still cultivating forty acres of cotton with mules—real mules…not Kawasakis. I remember one day during the fall of 1965, Uncle Vernon came home from the field early and staggered to the back porch steps where he stopped to take a swig from a mason jar full of white lightning which he had no doubt bought from my father. I know this happened exactly as I am relating it because I was there helping my cousin Larry put new tin on the smoke house. He hollered at his wife, "Spar, I'm bringing Roo (that was the mule's name) into the kitchen." (Spar was my aunt's nickname. No one knows where she got it.) Aunt Spar was like an old shoe; everything was worn out except her tongue, and on this day it was more potent and poisonous than a timber rattler. She waxed eloquently at the rate of 280 words per minute with gusts up to 350 in the language she was most fluent in, southern profanity. I can still recall almost all the cuss words she threw at him that day. It was like the Rebs shelling Fort Sumter to get the Union Army out of our fort. She let him have it with both barrels. "You crazy, drunk, redneck reprobate, you're about as worthless as a one-holed button. You take that stinking mule and go back to the field." Uncle Vernon didn't listen. He marched ole Roo up six back porch steps into the kitchen and paraded him around the kitchen table. (I think he did it seven times, just to make it an event of Biblical proportions.) Cousin Larry was four years older than me, and weighed almost 235 pounds at the tender age of sixteen. He was stronger than Hoss Cartwright but not quite as ugly. Best I remember, he tossed Uncle Vernon over his shoulder like a sack of feed and led Roo out of the house and put them both in the barn where they belonged. Roo stayed there for the rest of his life except when he was plowing. Uncle Vernon only had to sleep there a week. Yes, many things must not be allowed in our homes lest they bring the filth and the stench of the barnyard and the world with them.

After we establish a good worship routine in the home, we must take it beyond the walls of our castle. After getting our souls energized by God's word and our hearts encouraged by our family's love and support, we must then suit up in the Armor of God, lower the drawbridge once again and go forth into the world to worship with other likeminded Christians. It doesn't end there. Christ tells us in no uncertain terms that we are then to take the message of God's love and free salvation to the whole world.

A word of caution here: what we do in the home and in corporate worship must be real in order for our efforts at evangelism to have any chance of success. If we are not real in our Christianity, our family will be the first to know it. If we show up at church about as often as Puxatawny Phil comes out to predict the weather, our fellow churchgoers will know it and in less time than it takes for the Waltons to say good night, we will be branded a "hypocrite." What's down in the well will come up in the bucket. I am reminded of a small five-year old boy who started crying on the way home from his little brother's christening service. His father asked him three times what was wrong. Finally, the boy replied, "That preacher said he wanted us to be brought up in a Christian home (more sobs), but I want to stay with you guys."

Barry Switzer, former football coach, tells the true story of Wendel Mosley, nicknamed Deadset, who was on his football staff while coaching in Oklahoma. The reason for Wendel's nick-name is interesting and funny. He wore a set of earphones that were not connected to anyone, which apparently meant that Coach Switzer did not need or want his input for any of the decisions that they would have to make during a game. Coach Switzer gave Wendel the headset and earphones to boost his ego so that his girlfriend in the stands would think he was directing the game and making the calls. Is this not a perfect illustration of hypocrisy? Don't many so-called Christians walk around with "deadsets?" If we are going to convince our kids, girlfriend, neighbors, or anyone of the sincerity of our faith, we better have "ears" on that are plugged into God's transmitter. Jesus said on many occasions, "He that hath ears, let him hear."

Another thing that is vital in the Christian home is discipline. As parents, we must learn tough love sometimes. Children are not always going to be obedient. Some are going to rebel and misbehave. At times they may even embarrass us. We must learn how to administer Biblically correct effective discipline. A few years ago there was much controversy over corporal punishment. I remember one of the main people against this type of discipline was Dr. Benjamin Spock, not to be confused with the science officer on the starship Enterprise. Actually, the long-eared Spock had a very effective form of discipline that he used on Klingons and anyone else that misbehaved known as the Vulcan pinch. He did not invent it however, because I remember my grandmother using it to bring me under control at a family picnic in 1962 which pre-dates Star Trek a few years. Dr. Spock advocated milder, alternative methods of discipline.

My mom did not believe in alternative methods like "time out," "sit in the corner," "go to bed without supper," or "you can't go fishing today." No, she believed in flogging. This was never more evident than on that day I put our tom cat in the refrigerator. Now the refrigerator was one of only two modern appliances we had, the other being the electric stove. It occurred to me on one hot blistering July day that old Tom was hot and needed cooling off. Actually, I wanted to scare my sister Elaine. My older sisters were known for doing mischief to me for entertainment. I decided it was payback time. I gathered ole Tom up from where he was sleeping on the back porch, and while my mom was busy at the clothesline hanging up the clothes she had just washed, I proceeded with my plan to cool him off by putting him in the fridge. Tom was not totally reconciled to the idea of being cooled off in this manner. I finally wrestled him in the little cold box amidst the buttermilk, butter, ketchup, and mayonnaise. The truth of the matter is, I had to offer him some left-over fried chicken that mom was planning to use for dinner that day. It worked. With the "cat in the bag" as it were, I went to the next room and waited for my unsuspecting victim, who I was certain would be my older sister, Elaine. (Sis, if you ever read this, please know that I am genuinely sorry for all the mean tricks I played on you during those days. I do, however, regret that on this occasion, you didn't get the furry party I planned for you.) I was well familiar with her habits and knew that she would probably want a glass of tea pretty soon. My plan backfired big-time. My sister was engrossed in reading a true story magazine and did not budge from the front porch rocker. My mom came back in from laundry duty and decided she wanted a glass of buttermilk. Before I could beat her to the refrigerator, she had opened the door and got a face full of a cold, damp, and very angry tom cat. The chase was on. I ran. Mom came in hot pursuit, buttermilk dripping from her hair and a little blood oozing from her nose where the cat had scratched her. She dogged me like Rosco P. Coldtrain dogged the "Duke Boys," "Why in the world did you put the cat in the refrigerator?" she screamed, as the chase continued. "It was Alvin's idea. (Alvin was my imaginary friend) He thought it would be cool to experiment with suspended animation, and ole Tom was the only volunteer we could find," I yelled, still running for my life. Needless to say, I got one of the worst floggings that day in the history of corporal punishment. I think she wore out two switches and called for my sister to get one of dad's old belts to finish the job. I got flora and fauna behavior modification that day. If Dr. Spock had showed up and intervened, Momma would have flogged him too. My mom was simply following the advice given by the writer of Proverbs, Chapter 13: 24, "He that spareth his rod hateth his son; but he that loveth him chasteneth him early." From that day forward, Mom wanted to have an instrument of behavior modification handy in case the peach tree died. A nail was driven into the wall beside the refrigerator with an old belt always hanging on it.

Finally, in order to assure we do a good job in the home and prepare our children for life, we must be sure to teach them the proper attitude toward others, toward God, toward themselves, toward things, toward life, and toward death. These values and attitudes must be taught to children while they are young because there is so little time between the child who is afraid of the dark and the teen-ager who wants to stay out all night. The following will be just some random thoughts about these attitudes in no particular order: no rhyme but plenty of reason—that is how I like to live my life.

First I'll share a childhood poem we have all probably heard:

> There was a crooked man, and he went a crooked mile;
> He found a crooked sixpence, against a crooked stile:
> He bought a crooked cat, which caught a crooked mouse, And they all lived together, in a crooked little house.

Did you ever wonder why everything in this poem had to be so crooked? Nothing was straight! Not animal, not mineral, nor plant. I think I see the wisdom of the poem today. The source of all the crookedness is in the first verse, "There was a crooked Man." How we view life begins with how we view ourselves. Just as we can see a rose as a beautiful flower with a thorny stem, or a dangerously thorny stem, with a flower on one end. So, too, can we see life as either a tragedy with occasional funny moments, or we can see life as a comedy with an occasional tragic moment.

As you may have guessed by now, I am a "Trekkie." I thoroughly enjoyed every episode of those old 'Star Trek' shows, and I love to quote Spock. He had this common sense thing to say about our attitude toward things, "After a time you may find that having is not so pleasing a thing after all, as wanting; it is not logical, but it is often true." Winning is not really important if we do not enjoy playing the game. If the only time a mountain climber enjoys his sport is when he reaches the summit, he is like a cat chasing his tail; he is in a fruitless pursuit. We must learn to enjoy the climb. We must learn to love people and use things, not the other way around. We must maintain an attitude of loose attachment to things because they are not permanent. Children, before their attitudes become corrupted by worldly greed and the obsession of possessions, have this free spirited, nonchalant attitude. If we observe them playing on the beach we will be amazed to see what effort and care they put into building a perfect sand castle. They are funny to watch as they contort their mouths around and stick their tongues into their cheeks striving in earnest concentration to get every detail of the turret and towers just right. Then a big wave approaches, but the kids don't panic; they don't whine; they don't complain. They do something very surprising. They jump up and down, scream with excitement, and actually enjoy the sight of the ocean water destroying what they had labored so painstakingly to build. No sadness, no hysteria, no bitterness. Even little tykes have the wisdom to know the inevitable fate that awaits sandcastles. Adults must learn this lesson and teach it to our children. Scriptures are full of what we have just learned. The stuff of this world is like the sandcastles on the beach: temporal, and about as permanent as a wisp of smoke or the morning dew. We can plan, strive, push and shove, compete, climb and claw our way to the top and amass a lot of toys, but, like the game of chess, at the end of the game, kings, pawns, and bishops, go back into the same box or like the game of Monopoly, Park Place goes in the same box with Baltic Avenue. We must teach children the difference between wealth and money. We must teach them that greed is bad, but some desires and pure ambitions are O.K. and necessary to keep life in motion. Further, we must show them how to enjoy what they have, be grateful for it, and be willing to share their blessings with others. We live very close together in this world, and as the population explosion continues, we will live even closer. Therefore, we should resolve that our highest purpose in life should be to help others. If we cannot help them, we should at least not hurt them. We need for them to understand that we live in a world of abundance, and it is all available to us if we seek it in the right way. "There was never a banquet so sumptuous but someone dined poorly at it."(French Proverb) This means that we are worthy to dine at the feast of abundance that God has provided for us. We are worthy to be at His table if He invited us, and we should never go away hungry. We should never feel unworthy like Groucho Marx felt when he said, "I would never join any club that would have me as a member." We are children of the King. We are a royal priesthood—a

Holy nation, and we can partake of God's prosperity if we follow the rules of prosperity.

One of my favorite sit-coms of the old days was "The Beverly Hillbillies." Of course, I had a crush on Ellie May and wanted to marry her. Donna Douglas, who played Ellie on the show, is a wonderful Christian witness for the Lord. I was fortunate enough to meet her not long ago and arranged for her to speak at one of the churches in Coffee County. She is even a better preacher than a wrestler. Anyway, on one of the earlier episodes, Jed and Pearl were having a discussion about the decision to move away from the mountains to downtown Beverly Hills. Jed asked, "Cousin Pearl, what d'ya think? Think we oughta move?" Cousin Pearl replied, "Jed, how can ya even ask? Look around ya. Yore eight miles from yore nearest neighbor. Yore overrun with skunks, possums, coyotes, and bobcats. You use kerosene lamps fer light and you cook on a wood stove summer and winter. Yore drinkin' homemade moonshine and washin' with homemade lye soap. And yore bathroom is fifty feet from the house and ya ask, "Should I move?" Jed replies, "I reckon yore right. A man'd be a dang fool to leave all this!" Teach your children to be thankful for and to appreciate what they have.

Another quote from my friend Captain James Tiberius Kirk, "There are a million things in this universe you can have, and there are a million things you can't have. It's no fun facing that, but that's the way things are." We must help our kids realize the truth in that statement and help them in the process of setting priorities in life. Once choices have been made we can pursue them all-out, never forgetting to ask God's guidance and always knowing "All things are possible with Christ Jesus." (Mark 10:27) Having a focused goal and a worthy guide in the Holy Spirit will keep us from going off half-cocked in pursuit of too many objectives. Like Stephen Leacock described a fellow, "He flung himself upon his horse, and rode madly off in all directions." If we want it all, we might wind up like a monkey who reaches his hand into a vase of candy but never gets to eat the candy because he will not unclench his hand. Learning to let go of secondary, unimportant goals will allow us to pursue the task at hand and complete it with success.

Sometimes we just gotta suck it up and face the world like the detective Phillip Marlowe did in an old movie; "I got up on my feet and went over to the bowl of water sitting on the table in the corner and threw cold water on my face. After a while, I felt a little better, but not much. I needed a drink; I needed a lot of life insurance; I needed a vacation; I needed a home in the country; I needed a new car. What I had was a coat, a hat, and a gun. I put them on and went out the door."

Probably the most important attitude that our children need to be taught is the attitude toward death. In teaching this, we will teach them about an unshakeable faith in the one who has conquered death. F.W.H. Myers relates the story of asking a man at a dinner table what he thought would happen to him when he died. "Oh well, I suppose I shall inherit eternal bliss, but I wish you wouldn't talk about such unpleasant subjects." Many, like this man, probably our children included, may not want to talk about this subject. "Eternity is a terrible thought," wrote someone else, "I mean, where is it going to end?" However, we must approach the subject using scripture as our aid to explain that we as Christians have nothing to fear about death. One of my favorite scriptures is II Timothy 1:7; "God has not given us the spirit of fear, but of power, and of love, and of a sound mind." Many people are in denial about death, but death is inevitable. As Oscar Wilde said, "One can survive everything nowadays, except death." No matter what terms we use to express it, death is a reality; Ralph Kramden explained it to his friend Norton on the day that he thought he was dying, "Well Norton, I guess there'll be no more bus rides for me. I've come to the end of the line. I'm going to that big bus depot in the sky. It's a one-way trip with no transfers." Floyd Lawson, Andy Griffith's barber, used the same metaphor, "The bus bringeth and the bus taketh away." You know, that's a lot like life.

The scriptures that assure the Christian of an eternal life in heaven are too numerous to mention here. Godly parents must first study these verses themselves and then explain them to their children. Stonewall Jackson, one of the South's great generals and a mighty warrior for the Lord as well, gave us some reassuring insights about death. After being mortally wounded by his own troops who mistook him for the enemy right after the battle of Chancellorsville, General Jackson had to have his arm amputated and later died from his wounds. These are the words he spoke to a Presbyterian pastor as he lay on his deathbed, "You see me severely wounded but not depressed; not unhappy. I believe that it has been done according to God's holy will, and I acquiesce entirely in it. You may think it strange, but you never saw me more perfectly contented than I am today. For I am sure that my heavenly Father designed this affliction for my good. I am perfectly satisfied that either in this life, or in that which is to come, I shall discover that what is now regarded as a calamity, is a blessing." His last day, May 10, 1863, found his wife Anna by his bedside. She too was a strong Christian and reassured her husband: "Before this day closes, you will be with the blessed Savior in His glory." Jackson said, "I prefer it." A few minutes later, he uttered his final words, "Let us cross over the river and rest under the shade of the trees."

Let us all resolve to strengthen our nation by first strengthening our homes. We can do this only by establishing a time of daily devotion, prayer, and Bible study. We must cleanse our homes of all things and attitudes that are offensive to God. We must hang a sign on our front doors that says, "As for me and my house, we will serve the Lord." Then, we must indeed, serve God faithfully and consistently.

CHAPTER IV

OUR TAX SYSTEM MUST BE REPAIRED OR REPLACED

Many years ago our forefathers rallied around the credo, "Taxation without representation is tyranny." After seeing tons of our tax dollars flushed down the toilets of special interests and foolish government programs, we have discovered that "taxation with representation" is not so good either. Our representatives have managed to take forty percent of every dollar we make and still conjure up new taxes every year. Like they say, "You can always count on death and taxes." However, death, unlike taxes, does not keep getting worse every year. Will history remember Obama as the "Great Accuser," "The Great Bankrupter," or the "Great Pretender?" I don't know how history will remember him, but I think if he made a guest appearance at some Indian Pow-Wow and they let him smoke the pipe with them, they would give him an honorary "Indian name." What would this name be? Well, it depends on which tribe he visits. I am of Machise Creek descent; my wife is a descendent of William Weatherford (Red Eagle). We have both agreed that his name should be "Dull Knife" because he has not cut government spending. He has not cut unemployment; he has not reduced the deficit; He just hasn't cut the mustard as a responsible president. Other tribes may come up with other names such as Lying Dog, Mocking Bird, Lazy Lizard, or Crowing Cock.

Mr. Obama has done some name-calling himself. He called Bush "irresponsible and unpatriotic" for increasing our national debt by $4 trillion dollars. That is indeed an awesome accomplishment for one president in just a few years, especially when we consider that it took the first 42 presidents to account for our first $5 trillion debt. In order to hide his own culpability for our present economic crises and tremendous debt, Obama continues to whine about "what Bush did," and "I'm still trying to undo what Bush did." I am not a Bush fan either. He also exceeded the limit on doing stupid stuff. But let me set the record straight. During the Bush administration America enjoyed six straight years of economic growth. Per capita after tax income increased by more than ten percent and there was at least a four percent increase in new businesses.

Our present president has lied to us. Somehow that sounds familiar doesn't it Richard and Bill? He continues to lie to us. He reminds me of a superintendent for which I once worked. On one occasion I was in conversation with a former school board member who had hired this guy after he left my county. Somehow, my former boss's name came up. Yea, I know. Small minds discuss things, really shriveled brains discuss people, and great minds discuss ideas. Well, on this day neither I, nor my friend had any ideas. We had no weather that day, so we just naturally sunk to the lowest level of conversation and talked about our mutual acquaintance. My friend said, "You know that administrator would rather climb a tree and tell you a lie than stand on the ground and tell you truth." Obama either likes to lie or climb trees or both because he is just like the guy I mentioned. He promised to save or create at least three million jobs by the end of 2010. It didn't happen. Unemployment has been around nine percent for most of his term. At the end of 2010, there were actually fewer jobs than when he took over the oval office. I am amazed by the millions of Americans who are not aware of the circus side show trickery that is going on year after year with our tax money. Our tax structure is nothing less than a program of exploitation and rip off of the few who do work hard in America. In the last years of a previous administration, I won't call any names for fear of offending all you democrats, but I will tell you that the facts I will share next probably happened when the president was distracted with a Monica project or something: Twenty-six thousand very special people received $8.5 million in food stamps. I call these people "very special" because they were all **deceased** at the time the food stamps were delivered. During that same period, the General Accounting Office of the United

States of America estimates (they don't ever have the exact figures because our government has too many wrinkles and the exact numbers get lost under them) that $100 million was mistakenly sent to Medicare recipients. Who is minding the store? Did we put the fox in charge of the hen house again? Government waste is appalling. Incompetence, negligence, apathy, and outright fraud permeate those pin heads on the Potomac like stink in a septic tank.

Wake up Americans! Wise up! Do your due diligence: get the facts, learn the truth, and speak up. Once we know the truth about all this we still won't be free; not yet, not till we come together and do something about our predicament. What is a predicament? The best definition I can give is "a frog on a freeway that has lost his hopper." That is where we find ourselves today. Can anything be done to fix our hopper or get a new hopper? Actually, there is: we must rid ourselves of all the rabid republicans and dysfunctional democrats. Some of these guys have never seen a war or new tax they didn't like. They are not watching our tax dollars. They have the notion that they were hired only to spend money. Most federal and state expenditures are designed to get votes. Congress allocates and ear-marks money, but we have no separate government department to regulate and oversee expenditures. The General Accounting Office is summoned only when there is suspicion of foul play, and by then the money is harder to find than Jimmy Hoffa, D.B. Cooper, or Amelia Earhart. Very recent examples prove my point. How, specifically, was the billion dollars spent that the Clinton administration sent to Haiti? Show me an itemized expense account of Hillary's unnecessary trip to North Africa, and where is the $5 billion that the Department of Agriculture can't find?

On one occasion, David Walker, the CEO of the Government's Accounting Office was asked the whereabouts of $450 million of educational tax money. Walker replied, "I can't tell you where the money is. We do know that the Department of Education has some fundamental financial management problems. They don't have adequate accountability." (Boy, that is an understatement!)

So, who is watching the flow of our tax dollars into society? Who is accountable for the success of all the federal programs for which our taxes are ear-marked? Is there a special congressional committee?

41

No one should be surprised that the answer to this question is "no." Trillions are being spent but no one watches the money. America is on the verge of bankruptcy because we have no accountability. What would Thomas Jefferson have said if he were given the evidence of such blatant waste and unaccountability? I think he would have been more shocked than when his mistress told him she was expecting. Ole Tom's sexual indiscretions aside, he did have a great idea for government accountability. Consider what he said to Albert Gallatin in 1802, "We might hope to see the finances of the union as clear and intelligible as a merchant's books, so that every member of congress and every man of any mind in the union should be able to comprehend them, to investigate abuses, and consequently to control them. Our predecessors (I think he was referring to the Adams' Administration) have endeavored by intricacies of the system and shuffling the investigation over from one office to another to cover everything from detection. I hope that we shall go in the contrary direction, and that by our honest and judicious reformation, we may be able to bring things back to that simple and intelligible system on which they should have been organized at first." Tom, old fella, we need you to visit our accounting office and do a little audit in America. We need a report on your conclusions and summaries in one week. Jefferson would probably take one look at the mess and conclude, "You boys are full of it. America does not have enough computers and mathematicians to unscramble this mess. Good luck, I'm outta here."

According to Thomas Jefferson, "Eternal vigilance is the price of liberty." What exactly did he mean by that? He means that if we have anything worth preserving we better keep an eye on it. Not only do we have to worry about drug crazed addicts stealing what we have today, but we also have to keep a sharper eye on the den of thieves in D.C. (D.C. by the way stands for District of Corruption.) Only something of great value needs constant security measures. Our blood bought American freedoms and liberties fall into that category. Many of our politicians do not place such great value on our American treasures and would sell out for personal gain as quickly and thoughtlessly as Esau sold his birthright for a fine dinner. How many of our elected officials have sold us out after being wined and dined and bribed by some large company's lobbyist? Unscrupulous individuals, trying to get ahead in the world, have purloined our privileges, lost our liberties, and forfeited our freedoms. Whoever was in charge of guarding our national treasures went to sleep and is guilty of dereliction of duty. Somehow, the fox has gotten into the hen house.

Starting immediately, we must tighten security. We must elect only responsible, honorable, and trustworthy men to be in charge of our national treasures. We Americans want and should demand leadership that can be trusted—someone like General Washington. Washington's Continental Army included French soldiers, Hessians, and a few Indians. He would not entrust the safety of his army or the fate of the revolution to anyone of questionable loyalty and dedication. When our small and ragged American army was in places of great danger, General Washington gave the following instructions, "Put only Americans on guard tonight!" That counsel is as wise today as it was then, and issues at stake are in no less danger of being lost.

The year was 1766, ten years before the revolution; the man was Benjamin Franklin, American statesman and one of the framers of our American government; the place…England, the mother country…The words spoken by that man to the British parliament was a warning; "If the Stamp Act is not repealed, the colonists might revolt." Men can only take so much. God Himself has said that He will not put more on us than we can bear. The British Parliament and the American Congress are not as kindhearted and considerate as God. Americans are paying over forty, yes forty, different taxes to support an unproductive bureaucracy whose members receive twice as much as the private sector's pay. In January, 2010, over 40,000 new laws and regulations went into effect enabling the growing bureaucracy to have greater control and to take advantage of the tax-paying middle class.

In the United States we have two legal ways to avoid paying income tax: One is to declare ourselves a sovereign citizen legally and two is to learn about "The Fair Tax" which Congressman John Linder of Georgia proposes and ensure that it becomes law in America.

Are you a slave or a free man? Did you know that there are, in this nation, two separate and distinct classes of citizenship? You can be either a federal citizen, exploited and taxed to death, or a citizen of the several states as described in the Constitution and represented by a life of joy, freedom, and sovereignty as intended by our founding fathers. More and more Americans are becoming educated on this matter of state citizenship and state sovereignty. Until 1866, U.S. citizenship did not exist. Even now citizenship is a hoax, a defacto status—another name for slavery. We Americans need to figure out our birthright, especially regarding taxes and the federal government. The 14th Amendment to the U.S. Constitution introduced the new class of citizenship. Pay very close attention to Article I, Section 4. The 14th Amendment is invalid. The amendment was never properly ratified, and it contradicts the original constitution. To verify this for yourself, read the Congressional Records, June 13, 1967, Page 15641, HCON Resolution 206 or 208. U.S. citizens, as defined by the 14th Amendment, have a social security number, use a zip code (which invokes federal jurisdiction), are required to file tax returns, and in essence, are no more than slaves. The constitution and the Bill of Rights do not protect them. State citizens are quite different; they are considered "sovereign" and have full protection of the constitution and the Bill of Rights. State citizens don't have a social security number and are not required to pay income or property taxes. They are not required to have a driver's license or tags on their cars. The government recognizes and treats them as sovereign.

According to the IRS Handbook, "Our tax system is based on individual self-assessment and voluntary compliance." However, because you are a U.S. citizen, you cannot simply stop paying taxes. Even though a jury has on rare occasions not convicted the non-filer, the courts, as a rule, will legally force the tax payer to pay because he is in a contract. We Americans have ignorantly gotten into contracts with the federal banking system and its collection agency, the IRS. Once in this contract we must abide by it. We initiated the contract when we first got our social security number and filed the first income tax return. This contractual agreement lowers our status to that of a 14th Amendment U.S. citizen or slave. We are in this oppressed condition and under contract because we allowed private bankers to create U.S. money instead of representatives of **we the people** through congress. The founding fathers of the U.S. constitution tried to prevent this in advance by authorizing only the congress to "mint our coin and regulate the value thereof." (Constitution, Article I, Section 8, Clause 5) John F. Kennedy tried to get us out of this mess with the big banks and the Federal Reserve System. For a short time some dollars printed did not say "Federal Reserve Note" on the bill. Could his stand against the Federal Reserve have anything to do with his assassination?

Anyone having an interest in becoming a sovereign citizen, must educate himself on the pros and cons of that move. It is not for everyone. Some still have a slave mentality. The most effective form of slavery is the one in which the slaves do not realize they are enslaved. John Adams said, "A nation that wishes to be ignorant and free, wishes something that cannot be."

The second way to avoid paying income taxes and many other taxes that burden Americans is to learn about the Fair Tax legislation proposed by John Linder, a Georgia congressman with some common sense. Then we must work diligently to get this bill passed into law during the next four years regardless of who sits in the oval office. This legislation is described in a book called <u>The Fair Tax Book</u>. Any citizen who is passionate about seeing positive change in America, should buy a copy of this book and read it. Congressman Linder has the most common-sense approach to tax reform ever proposed in America. This workable plan would certainly have life-changing implications for all Americans if it were enacted into law.

The corrupt and complicated tax codes in America have allowed unscrupulous law-makers to "shaft" Americans for over 200 years. This can mean two things: the lawmakers get the gold mine and, "we the people" get the empty shaft or we get the wrong end or the short end of the stick. The relevancy of this last term will become very apparent when I tell you the origin of the phrase. The Romans were very concerned about personal hygiene, but they did not have indoor plumbing in their private homes. They had to use public facilities to relieve themselves and to clean up after the relief. For this clean-up the Romans used what I call a large one-ended Q-tip. (They did not have corn cobs or Charmin.) They left this stick or shaft in a pot of soapy water. Now some of the Roman senators, being distracted by thoughts of voting themselves a raise at the next session of the Roman senate, did not pay too much attention to how they returned the wiping stick to the pot. These almighty senators did not care too much about the next person in line for the potty. Needless to say, often times the wrong and messy end would be sticking up for the next person. I think we can all imagine the results of such thoughtless carelessness. When you got your last pay check, did you feel just like the next guy in line? Are you still trying to recover from getting "the wrong end of the stick?"

This fierce, fire-breathing dragon of unfair taxation can be slain. I must tell you about one of my favorite songs of the 60s' to show you how we can rid ourselves of this menacing monster. Peter, Paul and Mary sang "Puff the Magic Dragon," a song about an imaginary dragon. Puff was the imaginary creation of a little boy named Jackie Paper. Together they would sail around the world taking on all its evils including pirates and other rogues. Like Jackie, I had quite a runaway imagination as a child. I had a fictional playmate named Alvin, not a chipmunk, but a boy like me. Alvin's name probably came to me from watching too much of the chipmunks on TV. Alvin was my constant companion and a very real help in times of trouble. He was to me what George W. Bush was to Obama-a scapegoat. I blamed everything on Alvin. He was my Tonto; I was his Kemo Sabe. He was my Beaver; I was his Wally. I used Alvin like the boys in D.C. use unsuspecting voters-to get what I wanted. Sometimes when I would ask for more cookies, my mom would question, "Haven't you already had about a dozen?" "Yes," I would reply, "but Alvin has had only four, and he wants some more."

I also mentioned his name when I got into trouble. My dad made his living in construction and therefore had a good supply of woodworking and general purpose tools. He cared for those tools like some hunters care for their guns. He kept them clean and oiled. Every tool had a place, and he would know immediately if one were missing or had been used. I, myself, was a brilliant engineer at an early age and was the designer and general contractor of many projects like forts and castles. I remember when I was around seven years old, Alvin and I had to construct a fort to protect us from an invading Mexican army. Construction required extensive excavation. Alvin was not much help. I had to do all the digging myself. For this purpose I selected one of dad's hole-diggers. Early on, I learned that a pint-sized seven-year old was not quite man enough to use this tool. The two handles kept popping my ears as I manipulated them. I decided that the only solution was to modify this awkward, oversized device, so that a seven-year old boy could operate it without beating his brains out. After finding the sharpest handsaw among my dad's tools, I proceeded to amputate both of the handles on those hole-diggers. Alvin and I really made a good fort that day. We also killed off all Santa Ana's troops, saved Davy Crocket, William Travis, and Jim Bowie—a pretty good day's work for one real hero and one imaginary sidekick. The day was fun and exciting, but the excitement was not quite over. The setting sun was a brilliant red just matching my dad's face as he exploded into a rage at seeing what I had done to his diggers. His words still linger in my ears like the lullabies my mother sang to me. "Who sawed off my hole-diggers?" (this is a very mild translation of what my dad actually said that day) "I really can't say, Dad. I don't want to falsely accuse anyone, but I think I saw Alvin with them at some point during the day. I didn't actually see him cut them off, but he did use the hole-diggers." Unfortunately for me, dad didn't buy it. Final chapter on this story reads "CHOBB." (For all of you who have not been "Chobbed," it means Cow Hide On Boys' Butt.) My parents practiced many forms of discipline—biblical, botanical, and zoological. My mom preferred using local flora as instruments of punishment like cotton stalks and peach tree switches. My dad preferred fauna, usually his cowhide belt. Of course, on those rare emergency situations when I needed immediate thrashing, dad has been known to pick up the nearest thing at hand like a fire poker which is neither flora nor fauna.

Getting back to Puff the magic dragon, my son Kyle and my daughter Jennifer have always tried to convince me that the song had hidden meanings involving smoking pot. I refuse to believe it. Peter, Paul, and Mary, may have smoked pot, but the song does not talk about "puffing" a dragon. It tells about "Puff" who was a dragon. Even if a dragon is a thing used to smoke pot, I still will not accept it. I realize that certain singers in the 60's did put hidden meanings in their songs, like the Beatles did with "Hey Jude." So, I still maintain my original conviction. I tell my children that they must be smoking something to come up with such a ridiculous idea. To me, this sad song is about a little boy outgrowing his imaginary friend. It strikes a chord in my heart because I never want to outgrow certain things in my childhood—good friends, a loving family, honest and patriotic leaders, and an America where no one is hungry and everyone has an equal chance to succeed. The song says "When Jackie Paper came to play no more, Puff that mighty Dragon sadly slipped into his cave."

Please try to understand. Even if you have never had an imaginary friend and find it hard to believe that anyone else could have one, they do exist. Sadly, they go away when we grow up. What we have to do, Fellow Americans, with the dragon of taxes, is simply to outgrow them! We just don't show up to play the game anymore. We tell our elected officials that we are tired of the present oppression and scourge of excessive taxes, and that we insist that they consider the "Fair Tax" legislation which is being proposed. If we can all show up to buy a Chic-Fil-A sandwich to show our support for a Godly man who has simply exercised his First Amendment right and spoken out against an ungodly practice, we can all show up to vote for a tax system that would finally free us from extortion and exploitation. I assure you, this dragon of high and unfair taxes can be slain. Most of you are shaking your heads and saying, "It can never happen." I promise you that if implemented, the fair tax will rid our country of the IRS and the income tax. They will be extinguished from the face of the earth never to raise their ugly heads again.

The income tax did not always exist. The crooked scheming of a lot of Democrats and a few Republicans who sided with them drafted this evil income tax plot. The success of their camouflaged legislation, however, depended ultimately on the stupidity and apathy of the American voters. Politicians have always counted on stupidity or at least gullibility at maximum levels. In this case, we the people did not disappoint them. Politicians have before and continue to pee on us telling us they are raining favors on us and arrogantly expect us to believe it. In the case of the income tax, that is exactly what happened. They did not just tinkle; they sent a deluge! The storm has hovered over us ever since, and they tell us, "Smile. Don't curse the storm. Learn how to dance in the rain." I don't know about you, but I am tired of dancing to their tune. Let's put someone else on stage with a fiddle and a new song. If the new leaders play a good harmonious tune, I think we would all be willing to pay our fair share of the fiddler's fee.

At this point, I would like to give you a brief history of how the income tax came about and then give you a book report on one of the greatest and potentially life changing books since Thomas Paine's Common Sense. The Fair Tax Book is written by Neal Boortz and John Linder. I know most of you would rather be watching a reality show on TV or reading your horoscope in the daily paper than reading a book on taxes. However, I assure you, this book is good reading. It is life changing. A lot more real than any TV show. This fair tax book will tell you how we can ALL survive on this Island called America without voting anyone off the island. (Of course, we may have to vote some of our blind, bird-brained guys out of Congress.) Not only will we survive if we implement this plan, but we will prosper once again. Once you know the unscrupulous manner in which the original, oppressive, and unconstitutional income tax became law, you will be even more willing to join a national effort to abolish it. To tear down or dismantle anything unless we have something better to replace it is not wise. In this case, we have an infinitely better plan which will allow us, as Americans, to once again enjoy life instead of being reduced to mere survival mentality.

December 7, 1941 will always live in the hearts of Americans as a day of infamy. February 12, 1913, the birth-date of the despicable Federal Income Tax, should be remembered as a day of tyranny. If we all study the fair tax system proposed by Congressman John Linder of Georgia and vote for it when it is proposed, the IRS, April 15th, Income Tax, and all the pain and misery associated with them will be like Margaret Mitchell's "Old South." They will be "Gone With The Wind." We might even declare April 15 as a national holiday and celebrate it as "Former April Fool's Day."

The early democrats and a few misguided republicans, adeptly using all the political schemes and smoke and mirror deceptions, pulled off one of the most sensational coups known to man in passing the income tax into law. Lies were made to sound like truths and caused "we the people" to believe them. No matter what the politicians tell you, the IRS is the scourge of America and your dreams of financial freedom can never be accomplished with the ball and chain of income tax clasped around your ankles. Please consider what T. Coleman Andrews, Commissioner of the Internal Revenue Service 1953-1955, had to say about the Federal Income Tax, "Congress went beyond merely enacting an income tax law, and repealed Article IV of the Bill of Rights by empowering the tax collector to do the very things from which that article says we were to be secure. It opened up our homes, our papers, and our effects to the prying eyes of government agents and set the stage for searches of our books, our vaults, and for inquiries into our private affairs whenever the tax men might decide; even though there might not be any justification, beyond mere cynical suspicion."

The income tax is bad because it has robbed you and me of the guarantee of privacy and the respect for our property given to us in Article IV of the Bill of Rights. This invasion is absolute and complete as far as the amount of tax that can be assessed is concerned. Please remember. Under the 16th Amendment, Congress can take 100 percent of our income anytime it chooses. As a matter of fact, presently congress is imposing a tax as high as 91 percent. This is downright confiscation, defined in any terms.

Income tax was conceived in class hatred, is an instrument of vengeance, and plays right into the hands of the communists. It employs the vicious communist principle of taking from each according to his accumulation, of the fruits of his labor and giving to others according to their needs even when those needs are the result of indolence or lack of pride, self-respect, personal dignity, or other attributes of men. The income tax is fulfilling the Marxist prophecy that the surest way to destroy a capitalist society is by imposing steeply graduated taxes on income and heavy levies upon the estates of people when they die. As matters stand, if our children make the most of their capabilities and training, they will become slaves of the government giving most of their income to the tax collector. People cannot pull themselves up by the bootstraps anymore because the tax collector gets the boots and the straps. The income tax is oppressive to all. It discriminates particularly against those people who prove themselves most adept at keeping the wheels of business turning, creating maximum employment, and maintaining a high standard of living for their fellow men.

Mr. Andrews had more to say based on his years of service to the IRS, "I believe that a better way to raise revenue not only can be found, but must be found, because I am convinced that the present system is leading us right back to the very tyranny from which those who established this land of freedom, risked their lives, their fortunes, and their sacred honor to forever free themselves…"

Folks, in America we have already achieved at least two of the ten things that Karl Marx said must be accomplished to create a true communist society—a heavy and progressive income tax (Progressive means the rate of taxation will continually increase,) and free education to all children in public schools. (A communist government likes this because it can ban God and the Bible from the schools.) In the Communist Manifesto another goal was to abolish all rights of inheritance. We have not yet fully complied with this goal; we do, however, have estate and property taxes.

Our federal government managed to survive in the early years with very few taxes on a few basic commodities: sugar, tobacco, alcohol, and a few others. The War of 1812 created a greater need for funds. Taxes were levied on luxury goods. People generally do not oppose taxes needed to protect our freedoms from invading armies. However, over the years the government has taken advantage of these patriotic feelings. The year 1817 was a pivotal year in our country's history. In that year, the U.S. scrapped all internal taxes. The government operated with money raised from import tariffs. Voices heard in our early constitutional conventions spoke loudly about keeping the size of the federal government small by letting at least ninety five percent of it be done at the state and local level. America was following the game plan during these first years of our republic. Too many of the fellows today were elected to office without reading the history books or the Constitution. They evidently lost sight of our founding fathers' intentions for a small federal government. The income tax dragon first emerged from his cave during the War Between the States. In 1861, Congress passed a bill assessing a 3% income tax on everyone earning between $600 and $10,000 a year. It was a graduated tax even then, because if an individual earned over $10,000, the rate jumped to 5%. You Yankees are a bad influence on us southern boys, as evidenced by the fact that the Confederacy had its own version of the dastardly dragon.

The next fact in the saga of the income tax dragon is really hard to believe. People grew tired of the income tax. They let their representatives know how displeased they were, and the smart congressmen in D. C. repealed the income tax and returned to taxing commodities. The dragon was once again in its cave. Sadly, he was only sleeping. He would wake up hungrier than ever. Over the next two decades, die-hard dragon lovers would introduce no less than 68 bills to bring back the dragon.

Skip forward to the year 1893. Big Grover Cleveland was in his second term, and the country was in the middle of what has become known as the "Panic of 1893." Railroads were going bankrupt causing a chain-reaction that soon collapsed many banks and small businesses which were dependent on the railroad. If you have studied history at all, you know that an economic panic, like a war, is a signal for congress to go coin hunting in our pockets. The next event that transpired would be exceedingly funny if it had not resulted in a permanent reemergence of our good friend, the dragon. I remind you. Our dragon is and always has been real, not imaginary like "Puff the magic Dragon." I remind you also that you slay both the same way.

By now, politicians realized the fact that not all voters were stupid. They knew if they proposed a bill with the words income tax in it, the people would catch on and never vote for it. Also, politicians in those days were not nearly so clever at making distasteful legislation more palatable by giving it a prettier name. For example, today if legislators want to introduce a bill that affects stupid kids, they don't say "stupid kids." They refer to them as "developmentally challenged" or "minimally exceptional." If someone gets fired from his real job, they will say, "He was transitioned out," due to downsizing. Their use of "sweetening words" has spread to all segments of our culture. I can't elaborate on all of them, but one more example is garbage collectors who are now called "sanitation engineers." Well, that's good because now a developmentally challenged kid can go to college and major in sanitation engineering. I'm like Larry the Cable Guy here, "Forgive me, Lord. I did not mean to offend anyone," for Lord knows, I was myself a developmentally challenged, stupid kid, but Alvin and I were good engineers, nevertheless.

Let us get back to the history of the income tax. In 1894, our boys on the hill knew that they had to come up with a way to slide the income tax package by the scrutiny of the American voters. So, they came up with; "An act to reduce taxation, to provide revenue for the government, and for other purposes." I agree with Neal Boortz on this one. He asked, "Just how much can you trust a politician who passes a law to tax your income and calls it an 'act to reduce taxation'?" I believe that such a blatant attempt to deceive the American people is genetically enhanced bull-butter. (bull-butter is a polite name for those piles of black stuff that you do not want to step in if you are walking in a cow pasture.) Can you believe that the writers of that bill were so developmentally challenged and lacking of creative use of the English Language? This new version of the tax would make every American making more than $4,000 pay two percent tax. Here's the kicker. Be ever mindful that a politician's first obligation is to himself. (They are experts on Shakespeare- "To thine own self be true."). They tacked on a little bit of pork, They decided that all government officials, state and local included, would be exempt from the tax.

At least one man involved in this proposal must have had some common sense and was not "minimally exceptional." His name was President Grover Cleveland. (Some of ya'll name your next male offspring Grover in his honor for vetoing this trashy piece of legislation). Actually, he did not veto it in the strict sense of the word; it became law without his signature. President Cleveland figured that the Supreme Court would surely rule it "unconstitutional." The Supreme Court decided the constitutionality of the bill just as President Cleveland had predicted—the income tax was declared unconstitutional.

We all know by now how tenaciously persistent politicians can be in cases which give them a chance to rob the people. The Democrats, who thought they could not live or function unless they got this money, called for a constitutional amendment which would permit the heretofore unconstitutional legislation. Republicans were opposed to the scheme in principle. The proponents of the income tax took advantage of a sentiment existing in the people then as strongly as it does today, called economic class warfare. The Democratic proponents of the bill appealed to the masses of poor and middle class Americans assuring them that the tax would soak the rich but the majority of Americans would be under an umbrella. In other words, in this rain of taxes, only the rich would get wet.

The next verse of this song called, "Dirty Politics" involves Joseph Bailey, conservative senator from Texas, who thought he could kill two birds with one stone. He conscientiously objected to the bill but could not publically oppose it lest he be branded a traitor against his own party. Bailey reasoned that the Republicans led by Rough Rider Teddy Roosevelt would swoop in and kill the legislation like they did the Cubans on San Juan Hill. He would have his cake and eat it too. The bill would be killed. Bailey would still be a popular Democrat, and the Republicans would have mud on their faces for killing a bill designed to protect the poor and tax the rich. Though he was really against the income tax, Senator Bailey actually introduced the bill. Whew! Politics gets complicated sometimes. Well, as one of my favorite poets Robert Browning said, "The best laid plans of mice and men go oft awry." Roosevelt and his rough riding Republicans actually came out in support of the bill. Conservative Republicans were in a state of hysteria. Members of their own party were going to support a tax proposed by the liberal Democrats. Their plan to sabotage the Bailey Bill was to agree to support the bill on income tax if, and only if, an amendment to the constitution was passed into law, thus legalizing an income tax. They thought that the possibility of three-fourths of the state legislatures ratifying such an amendment would be slim, to none. Friends, they were wrong! Very wrong! Their gamble resulted in the passage into law one of the worst pieces of legislation in the history of government. The amendment zipped through the House and Senate like an Alabama running back through a Penn State defensive line. The vote in the senate was 77 to 0, and the House approved it 318 to 14! This bill was on its way to the states for final approval. The Democrats swarmed over their constituents like ugly on Van Gough. (Van Gough was not really ugly; he was "appearance challenged.") They went for broke in trying to birth this baby. The little black slave girl Prissy in <u>Gone With The Wind</u>, after having bragged about how much she knew about delivering babies, panicked when the opportunity actually presented itself. Prissy screamed, "Ms. Scarlett, I don't know nuttin 'bout birthin no baby." Well these Democrats were experts in obstetrics, especially with the birthing of bills with which they had been laboring for so long. They went to every soapbox in the cities and every stump in the country singing the praises of this bill. According to politicians, most Americans, especially in the West and South, would not be affected by the bill since incomes in these regions were rarely high enough to be taxed. Regrettably, "we the people," having been professionally mesmerized, hypnotized, and brain-washed, allowed this nasty little 16th Amendment to become law on February 12, 1913.

A degree of truth existed in what proponents had said about this income tax. During the first years of its implementation, only one-half of one percent of Americans actually paid any income tax. That would change and change fast. Remember. This was a progressive income tax. Those poor souls who had believed that only the rich would ever feel the cruel reality of the misery of this tax, would suddenly, like new born puppies and converted heathens, have their eyes opened. Soon the average American would have to struggle to feed, clothe, and educate his family. Friends, it will get worse! We are approaching the "tipping point" of this tax situation.

The federal income tax has accomplished what the liberal Democrats who instigated it wanted. This tax has escalated class warfare in America so that politicians can use it as a bargaining tool in the election and legislation processes. More and more Americans have become dependent on the government for subsistence. This tax bill finally led to the adoption of with-holding taxes, which allows the government to get its hands on our money before we see it.

This all came about because of another war and more propaganda—this time, using none other than Donald Duck as a spokesman for the cause. I do not wish to address the history of the practice of with-holding taxes. I have given you enough history of corrupt manipulation and deception of the American people by its elected officials to stir you to action. If you are interested in Donald Duck's part in this tax becoming law, research Walt Disney's animated cartoon called, "The New Spirit." If you went to a movie in 1942, you might have seen the cartoon. Disney studios produced the cartoon at the request of the Treasury Department to help the war effort and to help congress get their hands deeper into our pockets. Both goals were achieved. We finally won the war, and the current Tax Payment Act of 1943 became law. Donald Duck with his slurred speech was able to have a dynamic effect on voters in 1942. I really hoped that Clint Eastwood with his stammering speech and "empty chair routine" would have had a similar great impact on voters in 2012.

Let me explain just a few things that the fair tax will and will not do. First of all, the fair tax is clear and easy to understand, the way Jefferson said a tax code should be. Using the fair tax code even "developmentally challenged" individuals like myself will be able to understand just what their tax obligations are and know when they are paying it. The simple code of the fair tax will do away with ten thousand pages of IRS rules and regulations. The Fair Tax will transform hundreds of pages of forms into worthless documents that can be recycled. Hopefully the former IRS agents who no longer have jobs can obtain employment at one of these recycling centers. If you want to discuss this legislation with your congressmen, you can refer them to the Fair Tax Bill Number H.R. 25 in the House of Representatives and S.25 in the U.S. Senate. Its official title is "The Fair Tax Act of 2005".

A long list of existing taxes will automatically be repealed when the Fair Tax is signed into law. Some of them include:

* The individual income tax
* The alternative minimum tax (AMT)
* Corporate and business income taxes
* Capital gains taxes
* Social Security Taxes
* Medicare taxes (along with all other federal payroll taxes)
* The Self-Employment tax
* Estate Taxes
* Gift Taxes

All those miserable and burdensome taxes will be replaced with a single-rate, personal consumption tax—a simple sales tax on new goods and services. You must understand at this point what the fair tax is not. The two statements that follow are extremely important in understanding the Fair Tax:

1. THE FAIR TAX IS NOT A VAT (Value-added tax,) similar to European VATs. VATs are added at every stage of production and hide tax costs in the price of goods. In contrast, the Fair Tax is levied once and only once-at the retail cash register, and it's printed on the sales receipt for all to see.

2. THE FAIR TAX IS NOT AN **ADDITION** TO OUR CURRENT FEDERAL TAXES: It is a **REPLACEMENT** FOR our current taxes. It's simply a new and equitable method for raising the same amount of money our old and complicated code raises today. Don't let anybody fool you into thinking this is a tax increase. Don't any of you fool your friends into thinking that it's a tax cut. This tax is neither. It is simply a common sense tax replacement.

According to John Linder, author of the Fair Tax, The Fair Tax Revenue is neutral. In other words, the sales tax rate will be set to ensure that the federal government and all the programs within it, including Social Security and Medicare, will receive from the national retail sales tax exactly what they had been receiving under the current tax system. This isn't about cutting spending or changing government benefits. This plan simply changes the way Americans fund their federal government.

Unlike Obama, I have given you what I said I would in this chapter, common sense solutions to our tax problem. Will you follow up on whichever tax plan appeals to you? I will end this discussion with a final summary of what will change **if** the Fair Tax is ratified:

We start collecting 100 percent of our earnings in every paycheck.

We all get virtual raises since payroll taxes are no longer siphoned from our checks.

We all start receiving monthly prebates equal to the amount of consumption tax we would be expected to pay on life's basic necessities.

We all start saving and investing without any tax consequences.

The prices of consumer goods and services remain essentially the same with the removal of the embedded taxes compensating for the added consumption tax.

American businesses return operations to their home shores.

The richest Americans bring their money back home where it helps fuel our economy.

Those operating in the underground and shadow economies finally start paying taxes.

You hear a voice you recognize as a former IRS agent as you pull up to the drive-through service window at McDonald's asking, "Would you like fries with that?" (Neal Boortz and John Linder)

The ball is in your court. I don't know what course of action you plan to take as a concerned American. I only hope that you will act in a positive manner very soon—for time is running out for us. If we do not fix America soon, I assure you that the Hunger Games or a much worse scenario will become a reality in the land we love.

CHAPTER V

WELFARE MUST BE REFORMED AND RENOVATED

Crop circles and the Bermuda Triangle are two things that have always intrigued me. I love puzzles, mysteries, and unexplained phenomena. Arthur Conan Doyle is my favorite author followed closely by Charles Dickens, and whoever wrote <u>The Count of Monte Cristo</u>, whose name escapes me at the moment. I am amazed by Sherlock Holmes' methods of scientific detection. I am ecstatic when I read the ending of <u>The Count Of Monte Cristo</u> and see the bad guys finally having to give an account of their lies, hypocrisy, and treachery. I like to see the good guys win. Using some of Sherlock's methods; I will try to assimilate the facts about this administration and maybe, as in <u>The Count of Monte Cristo</u>, the bad guys will have to answer for their crimes and the good guys will win.

Two other geometric forms come into play here. Let's forget about the crop circles and Bermuda Triangle for now. Let's concentrate on the Oval Office and Pentagon. Obama's give-away programs and entitlements, as they have come to be known, are more frightening than the thought of a giant asteroid hitting the earth and destroying life as we know it. In addition, his unforeseen and foolish cuts in defense spending are even more alarming. The odds of the earth being hit by a rogue asteroid are very slim, according to most astronomers. On the other hand, the chance of America being destroyed by "**spending on steroids**" is an absolute certainty if we continue on our present course of unaccountable and reckless spending.

David Walker, comptroller general in the U.S. Government Accounting Office, in a testimony before the House Ways and Means Committee, stated that if our discretionary spending remains at its current percentage of the total economy, by the year 2040, the entire federal revenue collected from all sources will not be sufficient to pay even the interest on the national debt. This means that there will be no funds for medicare, social security, defense, education, or any other government programs.

When we get rid of the smoke and mirrors of Obama's magic show and examine the true facts, we can see the deficits in the Bush days, especially when both the wars in Iraq and Afghanistan were at full throttle, were only a fraction of the unparalleled spending and consequent deficits the Obama Machine created. None of us can escape the laws of accounting. Spending on steroids leads to the disease of deficits, cured only by terrible taxes. Like the absurd, unscientific eighteenth century practice of bleeding with blood sucking leeches, the cure is very often worse than the disease.

Obama's plan might work if he had a magic lamp in his pocket to rub and coax a money genie to appear with billions of greenbacks. If he did have a genie and if he were given only three wishes, he would probably screw that up. Obama's first wish would probably be; "I wish all those republicans would disappear and never come back," Second, "I wish Oprah, the Kennedys, and the Jewish democrats would leave me alone and quit bugging me about having dinner at the White House to give me their slant on things." Third, "I wish Fox News and all those anti-democrat talk show hosts would quit telling the truth about me on national TV." Unfortunately, although he is a master of deception and illusion, Obama does not have a magic genie, or money machine or does he? Maybe he and Clinton do have access to Fort Knox. Maybe they have been sneaking in stealing the real gold bullion and replacing it with bogus bars of gold-plated tungsten, which has the same density or specific weight as gold. No, the only money machine Obama has is the American taxpayer. This machine is taxing almost everything in America today. Even our Olympic gold medal winners have to pay taxes on their trophies, just another way the baboons in congress discourage success.

Now, Let's talk about "entitlements." We have many legal classifications in America today: **legally blind, legally dead**, and **legally drunk**, to name a few. America has a very big problem with millions of lazy, no account folks who have declared themselves **legally unfit to work** or **legally lazy**. Democrats convince them that they are "entitled" to this free money for which the rest of us work hard. Legally, the term "entitlement" refers to something given to you through the proper process of law. Webster says it means, "To name, to give title to, to qualify, to fit for, and to give claim to." The only entitlement I knew about before the Obama democrats redefined it was a deceased person legally left his estate to his designated heirs through his will. Now, the heir might be a no-account, pot-smoking, lazy scumbag who drives a 1949 Ford tow-truck and hunts people who have made a wrong turn; but he is legally entitled to the estate. If Queen Elizabeth, hearing about what a really nice person I am, how much I love England, and that my ancestors were loyalist during the revolution, summons me to London to "knight" me, then my title henceforth would be, "Sir Ken." I would be "entitled." I can see it clearly in my dreams, Sir Ken announcing to my wife, "Honey, I am not going to do anything today or ever again. I am not going to take out the garbage, bring in the groceries, or anything else. "Why is that dear?" (For the record, we don't refer to each other as honey and dear. It's too much like Ward and June Cleaver.) "I have just received my knight-hood certificate in the mail. It is now official. I am a bona-fide, queen—dubbed, certified knight." "I am now Entitled." "Well, Sir Ken, Go on out and mow the grass or the first time you suit up in armor I'll have Hubert Ray come over and do a mig-weld on you." (For those of you who don't know Hubert Ray, he's our family welder.) Now, that is only a hypothetical situation. That did not happen and is not likely to happen, especially since I don't even keep up with who is on the throne over there. However, I will share with you a true example of entitlement that, legend has it, actually did occur. In 1617 King James I of England enjoyed a cut of loin so much that he dubbed it, "Sir Loin," hence the name of our popular cut of beef today known as sirloin. For those of you who watch Jeopardy and know the facts, James I, was flaky enough to have knighted a cut of beef.

Our great country is very likely to go bankrupt if our government does not stop the ridiculous practice of "knighting" and "entitling" so many people and groups of people. My common sense solution to this problem comes from the Apostle Paul. In Second Thessalonians, 3:10, he said, and I translate, "If you don't work, you don't eat." The only exercise millions of Americans get is their monthly walk to the mailbox or their drive in their Lexus to the post office to pick up their "entitlement." Maybe we need to add another legal classification; legally stupid. This "entitlement" would be for all those idiots who keep giving away our hard-earned tax dollars to healthy people who will not work. Once a law-maker is "knighted" with this title, we automatically retire him without a pension or better yet, we exile him to Elba. No, not the island Elba where Napoleon was exiled; but, to the south Alabama town of Elba, my home town. Having to make a living for his family in such a small town, he would learn to vote in a way that honored his commitment to his constituents. Unfortunately, congressmen are probably immune to early retirement laws. We can't just oust them from office. Why is it difficult for them to break the law? For one good reason, they make the laws. We need to wise up, America. They are hired hands! They work for us! We should set their salary and have some input into policing their behavior. Alas, their first agenda as law-makers is to take care of number one. They know that they must first pass legislation to either make them exempt from the laws that apply to the common man, or they enact laws that legalize whatever crooked scheme they plan to initiate once in office.

I can't think about "entitlements" without the true story of Eugene Carver coming to mind. Now Gene worked for my good friend Todd Flanningim who had a big farm in Coffee County, Alabama. I reckon Gene thought Todd was not paying him enough, so he asked him if he qualified for what we call in south Alabama, a "crazy check." Mr. Flanningim said, "I don't know Gene, but I will take you down to the welfare office and we'll see". At the interview Gene was asked, "Mr. Carver, when did you get married?" He answered, "The same year Mr. Todd got his divorce." "Mr. Carver, When is your birthday?" Gene replied, "It's this year." I'm pretty sure Eugene Carver got his "entitlement" that day.

Another urban legend that circulates in Dixie is that of poor old Mr. Isaac Benjamin Fertil. Everyone called him I.B., and I shall do the same. He was a widower with eleven children living in a run-down tenant house near the Pea River. Now I.B. Fertil had never been known for being a zealous worker. In fact, I can't remember anyone who had ever seen him in the field plowing or doing any kind of physical work whatsoever. His wife had just recently expired from a combination of excessive childbirth and improper hay stacking. The day after giving birth to their eleventh child, Mrs. Fertil suffered blunt force trauma to her whole body when a cat, having been kicked by the cow she was milking, landed on a stack of poorly stacked hay, causing twenty five heavy bales to bury and smother her to death. The whole community mourned this good woman's demise. Even old I.B. was sad because he knew that for the first time in his life he might have to do some work. Being a savvy old buzzard, I.B. tried to figure a way out. He had heard of certain government programs, (They were not called "entitlements" in those days.) So, he put in a request for the county welfare agent to visit. When Fern Gladys McElroy (Her initials as you can see, stand for Free Government Money) got to the Fertil farm, she immediately took out her record book and began asking questions: "What are the names of your children, Mr. Fertil?" I.B. began to name them: "Sarah, Rebecca, Ruth, Jacob, Isaac Jr., Daniel, and oh, little Esther." Then, while he caught his breath, the government lady said, "Is that all?" I.B. answered, "Oh no, them's just the Old Testament children. I've got several New Testament children. Let's see. I got Mary, Martha, Matthew, Luke, and John." "But that's twelve", quipped Mrs. McElroy. "Oh, that's right," replied I.B. "John was just in the planning stage at the time of the accident." As Fern wrote more notes in her little book, I.B. Fertil impatiently asked her, "Well, what do you think, Fern? Do I need assistance?" Fern hesitated for a minute, took a deep breath, and uttered, "No, Mr. Fertil, what you need is an operation!" Folks, it does not get any plainer than that. What we need in America is a major operation. We need some serious surgery performed on our national budget. Entitlements must be cut out and thrown away like an infected appendix.

Former president Clinton signed a welfare reform bill which would actually require people to get jobs. Obama wants to repeal the work clause of that legislation and allow states a waiver to the work provision which would in Obama's words, "thus allow for the testing of alternative and innovative strategies designed to improve employment outcomes." Spoken like a true lazy politician who has never had to work. My "common sense" response to this is: No alternative and innovative strategies will work better than work! We have no substitute for hard and honest work. Believe me. I tried every innovative and alternative strategy that a country boy could think of to get out of those hot dusty cotton fields. From the time I was big enough to drag a cotton sack, I was ushered to a field of white, fibrous bolls and told: "If you don't work, you don't eat." I believed it and started picking! The sun was hot; the earth was parched, and the gnats swarmed around me like Sherman attacking Atlanta. Nevertheless, I received no waivers, no opt-out clauses, and no entitlements.

Groucho Marx said, "Outside a dog, a book is man's best friend; inside a dog, it is too dark to read." We need to teach our children many things today, not the least of which is how to read. The Bible is the first book we need them to read. From the Bible they will learn among other things, a good work ethic and hopefully a lot of other ethics. From this book our children will learn the importance and rewards of work. From Esau and Jacob, they will learn that their future and entitlement can be lost in one hungry buying spree. From the prodigal son, our children will learn that if they want to party at their parents' expense and not work, they will end up dirty, lonely, hungry, and homeless. From the parable of the sower, they will learn that they must plant seeds and cultivate the tender plants in order to reap a harvest. Consider what R.G. Le Tourneau had to say about work, "When should a child start to work? I would say at about the age of three. I do not believe in the sweat shop or in child labor that deprives a child of his education or the pleasure of carefree hours and that breaks down his health and stunts his development. However, one thing is certain. If one does not learn to work as a child, he will never do much when he grows up. As for health, I probably sawed as much wood as a boy and shoveled as much sand in the foundry when I was in my early teens as the next fellow. I don't know what it means to lose a day through sickness. Can anyone show me a man today at the head of affairs who didn't work as a boy? I think that without exception, those who get things done today are those who learned to work as children. We need to teach our children the dignity of labor and the pleasure of accomplishment and that only by determined effort do we create things that are worth-while. Not only do sweat and toil keep us out of mischief, but the more we do, the bigger kick we get out of what we do."

We cannot go forward with a president or a government that insists on addicting the population to hand-outs and freebies. It is like a drug dealer giving a teen-ager his first dose of dope for free, just to try. After that first freebie, it is almost impossible to break the addiction. America is overrun with drug and alcohol addicts...a problem which creates plenty of havoc and costs us millions of dollars a year not to mention the tragic loss of lives. Addicting people to a "no-work mentality" will intensify the existing problem of drugs and alcohol which is already out of control. Whether you are a democrat or republican, we have no alternative to the old maximum, "an honest day's work for an honest day's pay." Right now, every American's share of the national debt is over $50,000.00. If we let Obama continue his policy of "Let the government take care of you," we will be well over $16 trillion dollars in debt by 2020. Perpetual motion is impossible as long as friction, inertia, and gravity exist, and I think these forces are here to stay. However, the democrats have figured out how to construct a perpetual "voting machine." Every time a baby is born to an unwed teenager who is already on welfare, we need to send the democrats a cigar. They just got another voter on their side. They have fifth and sixth generation voters already and as long as we pay people to have children, I am afraid the cycle will continue. Every time we allow illegal aliens to become part of our government assistance programs, the machine runs faster, churning out even more voters for those congressmen who continue to give out entitlements.

Letting Obama continue to pilot our ship is like letting Captain John Smith pilot the Titanic. Yes, Captain Smith was a smart man, but because he ignored the warnings of others and was not on the bridge when he was really needed, his mighty ship sank, costing the lives of a lot of men, women, and children. What is the common sense thing to do? Let someone else pilot our ship. Obama has had every chance to do right, fulfill his campaign promises, and set a practical course for America. He has had the luxury that not many presidents have had-serving with a congress that consists of a majority of his own party. Under Clinton, who served with a republican majority, 22.5 million jobs were created. Obama and his democratic congress have managed to lose almost 475,000 jobs since 2010. Under Obama, unemployment has remained above eight percent for 41 straight months.

As we conclude this chapter on entitlements, government waste, and corruption, I have just one common sense question. How in the world are we going to pay for all this? To balance our out of control budget, we would have to tilt the planet. I can think of only two things at present that could generate any serious cash flow into our coffers.

The first thing we could do is sell off some real estate. That's what France did when they were strapped for money. Remember the Louisiana Purchase. That's how we got Louisiana. France needed the money; we needed more territory. We haggled over price a little while and finally closed the best deal since we had bought Manhattan from the Indians for a few beads and trinkets. We could begin by selling Hawaii, which is too far away for most of us to enjoy anyway. I went to Hawaii in 1986 on business. I didn't feel welcomed. The natives there called me a "Houli." After all, what have we to lose? Those who can afford to fly could still visit. Next, we could sell California with the stipulation that the whole state had to be moved within two months from the purchase date. If the San Andreas Fault is not fixed, we are likely to lose California anyway, so why not go ahead and sell it? If that does not raise enough money to get our fat out of the fire, we could then consider selling all the duplicate states. You know, states like North Dakota, South Dakota, North Carolina, South Carolina, Virginia, and West Virginia. I don't recommend selling both parts, just the Northern parts, like North Dakota and North Carolina. I guess as a descendant of a rebel colonel, I still have an aversion for Yankees. That's why I suggest selling only West Virginia. I still have not forgiven you guys. We really needed you when we seceded.

Second, if enough funds are not raised through land sales, we could then resort to blackmail. This would not be a problem because our wits, half-wits, and dumb-wits at D.C. could coin another word that would sound better and would not technically be illegal. We actually could "white-mail" some other country. Surely you knew that there was such a thing. In sixteenth century England "mail" meant rent or tribute. White-mail was a debt paid in silver. Black-mail was paid in any other medium from grain to meat. White-mail had a set value; black-mail did not, allowing the one to whom it was owed to extort more than the actual debt. (Boy. That fits right in with how governments and their agents work.) So, here's the deal we offer any other country except Israel. (We must remain friends with these guys; therefore, we cannot do anything to upset them or their God.) "If you do not pay us 22 trillion dollars and have it counted out in neat stacks and placed at the base of the Lincoln Memorial by next Tuesday, we, the U.S. of America, by unanimous consent, will deliver Hillary Rodham Clinton, Barack Hussein Obama, Jeremiah Wright, and Joe Biden to your shores with instructions that they can never return to America.

If our tax dollars were being spent strategically and efficiently to create jobs, solve social problems, and safeguard our homes, I would have no reason to complain. But alas, that is not the case. Government waste is astronomical. Scams, cons, and frauds invade D.C. like Los Angeles fog. Corruption flows out of our seat of government like lava out of an erupting volcano with twice the damage. I fear that this corruption will only get worse since the Supreme Court's ruling in 2010 that corporations could spend unlimited sums of money to sway elections, thus equating corporate money with free speech. How much worse can things get? Our elected officials break the rules, circumvent the Constitution, and gerrymander their districts. Now they have the Supreme Court's approval to allow their special interest groups through large corporations to buy votes for them.

The two solutions I mentioned previously were just in fun. However, if common sense solutions to our economic crisis and other serious problems are not found soon, we may have to resort to solutions just as ludicrous, but we won't be laughing. I am convinced that if our great nation, with the limited technology of the time, could put a man on the moon in 1969, we can effectively solve the problems that confront us in 2012. The qualifications for being an astronaut are very strict. The men have to be in perfect health and have great vision. I think some of the same qualifications need to apply to our law makers. The common sense solution for America's problem is to find leaders with common sense, honest hearts, unselfish motives, and a clear vision for America that includes a faith in the God of this universe and a new commitment to His laws.

In my opinion, the fiscal soundness of our nation can only be secured by abolishing many of the entitlements we already have and certainly not creating any new ones that we cannot afford. Children, from an early age, must be taught the value and responsibility of honest labor. Children in all schools must be taught that it is not the government's responsibility to take care of citizens who are physically and mentally able to work. We must use common sense, and realize that tax-paying, hard-working citizens will eventually grow weary of supporting those who will not work, and will revolt.

CHAPTER VI

EDUCATION MUST BE REASSESSED AND REINFORCED

I am disturbed about the state of education in America. I am not the first to be concerned with this issue. On one occasion former President Bush asked, "Is our children learning?" The answer is "No Mr. President, they isn't." A more realistic, relevant, and grammatically correct question that needs answering is; "Are our teachers teaching?" I think that if we can fix just some of the problems that plague our educational system, we will be closer to solving other problems in our society. Of course, we have too many anti-education people in our world. Even members of congress are anti-education.

Knowing what they know will explain why they are against a good education for all the people. Do you remember that at one time it was against the law to teach a slave how to read? People in charge knew that it is nearly impossible to enslave a society of educated people. I firmly believe that if we can educate our masses in the right manner, they will never again be taken in by the lies that many politicians tell. Aristotle wisely observed, "All who have meditated on the art of governing mankind have been convinced that the fate of empires depends on the education of youth."

When we consider some of the recent educational statistics, we will realize that America is a scary place to live. The world is indeed scary; knowing that one man is carrying around a little "football" with which he can initiate a nuclear war, a large asteroid could wipe out most of the planet's population in a heartbeat; global warming might soon melt all the arctic ice and a lot of our coastal cities would be destroyed; and a vicious bacteria or virus for which we have no vaccine could spread across the U.S. and kill most of us in a week. Even though I have not even begun to scare you, I will proceed with the really frightening statistics. Forty-four million Americans cannot read and write above a fourth-grade level. Those who can read, spend only ninety nine hours a year reading a book and only eleven percent of Americans bother to read a daily newspaper, not counting the comics and the want-ads. Not only are we ignorant, but we apparently have no desire to learn. What is really scary is that in recent years we have endured a president who rarely reads anything including his own briefing papers. National math and science scores have flat-lined since 1971. Among the thirty developed countries, the U.S. is ranked twenty fifth in math and twenty first in science. By 2020 the United States will have an estimated 123 million high-paying, high-skill jobs. However, only 50 million Americans will be qualified to fill them. The percentage of children who read well has not improved substantially in twenty five years (NAEP 1996 Trends Report).

Knowing where we rank among other developed countries and considering all the aforementioned dismal educational statistics, should our nation be assuming the role as world police and flying around bombing places? Certainly not, as least not until the majority of the population learns to find Afghanistan on a world map and spell Libya correctly.

Now don't get me wrong, Americans are not stupid, especially when it comes to sports statistics. Just listen to any sports talk show, and you will be totally blown away with the knowledge of some of these guys. They can tell you who was on second base in game one of the 1962 World Series in the top of the seventh inning, what his number was, his batting average, and what he liked to drink after the game. I must put in a plug for the sports fans of the University of Alabama. They are some of the best if you don't count the one that went into tree poisoning as a hobby. If you listen to Paul Finebaum's weekly radio show, you will have to be impressed with some of their recall of the statistics pertinent to Alabama's great games. They know exactly who tackled who in the 1964 national championship game to stop the opponent from gaining a crucial first down, how much he weighed, what high school he came from, what his A.C.T. score was, whether he went on to play pro football and which cheerleader he dated. Well, give us credit. All our heroes have been cowboys or football players. We have had very few statesmen that we could follow as role models. There is nothing wrong with being a sports enthusiast and nothing wrong with remembering all these stats. All this verifies that the minds of Americans are a sharp as ever when it comes to things in which they are interested. I think we would have a better America if we would educate ourselves about what our leaders are doing and compare their voting statistics like we do batting averages of our favorite sports heroes. Then remember these figures when we go to the voting houses.

Recently a group of 556 seniors at fifty-five prestigious American universities (e.g., Harvard, Yale, Stanford) were given a multiple-choice exam consisting of thirty four questions that were rated at high school level. These top students could only answer fifty three percent of them correctly. Forty percent of those students did not know when the Civil War took place. The two questions that the college seniors scored highest on were; who is Snoop Dog? And, who are Beavis and Butt-head? Can you explain this? Why is our educational system in such shambles? Why are our educational institutions turning out such inept, ill-prepared, and ignorant products? I certainly do not have all the answers, but as I have already stated, it could be because of a conflict in the priorities in our educational budgets. I taught school for over fifteen years; therefore, I can testify to what I saw when I walked into most public schools. (By the way, Obama sends his kids to a private school. Maybe no public schools are located within driving distance of where they live. I don't know.) Where I taught public school I saw overcrowded classrooms, demoralized, unmotivated and underpaid teachers, leaking ceilings, outdated and ragged textbooks, overpaid and over staffed administrations, watered-down curricula, and well- watered football fields. I'm gonna be real with you boss...In south Alabama, if it comes to a decision of whether to give the science teacher water to drink or to water the grass on the football field, well, I'll let you guess who will be thirsty. America, here's your sign: "Just maybe the dumbest country on earth." We will continue to have problems turning out smart graduates from our high schools and colleges as long as we consider it a higher priority to build bigger and better football stadiums than to educate our children.

Another common practice in education that does not make sense is overloading teachers with an unmanageable teacher/pupil ratio. This problem definitely needs fixing. Of all the in-school factors that affect student achievement, effective principals and teachers account for nearly sixty percent of a student's ability to succeed. The number of students thrust upon them at one time greatly influences a teacher's effectiveness.

Teachers, bless their hearts, have always had to do so much with so little that most of them are now qualified to do everything with nothing. I remember my first few days at Rawls Elementary School in the piney woods of south Alabama. I was so excited. I thought I already knew everything and was all set to teach Ms. Faulkenberry some stuff she probably didn't know. After only two days she informed me that I was no longer going to be in the first grade. I was going to the second grade. I got really excited hearing this revelation. I somehow knew it would not take them long to recognize true genius once exposed to it. When I got to the second grade room, I found that my other seven or eight fellow first graders were already there waiting for me. Talk about a revelation! I was confused to say the least. The new plan I found out was to combine the first and second grades and use only one teacher to teach both grades. Actually I was relieved that they had not discovered that I had a retention deficit issue or some other derogatory label that would follow me throughout my educational career. I think this plan worked out well because we had so few students in both grades. Mrs. Myra Benton was such a dedicated and caring teacher that she was able to multi-task and as Larry the Cable Guy says, "Get-R-Done." In a lot of schools, however, such consolidation results in too many students for one teacher to control much less teach effectively. I can speak from personal experience on the issue of overcrowded classes. Many times I have been assigned at least eighty five boys and girls ranging from seventh-graders to seniors to instruct in physical education. Even in P.E. classes, teaching that many students effectively, and ensuring maximum learning for every pupil is difficult to impossible.

Another matter that our educational leaders might consider applying, at least a smattering of common sense to, is lowering standards at every level of the educational process. A net learning deficit among many of our high school graduates has resulted. I remember something that Billy Graham said that might drive this point home. A bunch of us rabid Baptist had driven to Birmingham to one of his crusades on a tranquil September night. I don't remember the sermon title. I don't remember how many got saved that night. I, typical of a lot of Southern Baptist, do not recall if I heard the entire discourse or slept through some of it. I do, however, remember the main point. I do believe it was educational in nature. Dr. Graham related how a coach at one of our "pride of the South" SEC schools was most eager for a certain football player to be accepted into the college. Entrance into our prestigious fortresses of higher learning was very rigid in those days. In the acceptance interview with the Dean of Admissions the prospective student was told that if he could answer only one question correctly, he would be admitted. The Dean asked, "What is the sum of six and six?" The student/athlete (more athlete than student) responded, "Thirteen." There was total silence for a few moments. Then before the Dean could say anything, the coach said, "Aw shucks, Dean, let him in He only missed it by two." I don't know. Maybe lowering our standards so that more students can matriculate might not be such a bad idea. I came to this conclusion after reading recently of how some high school seniors responded to questions on a survey. One girl, when asked if she knew what the Holocaust was, responded, "A Jewish Holiday." Statistics show that a large portion of today's high-school students don't know that Mexico is our immediate neighbor to the south. What is the answer to our pitiful state of education? Some bright nerdos are saying, "We need more computers in the classroom." I really believe that some teachers think that the more computers they have, the less they will have to teach. Just park that kid in front of the Dell and show him where the mouse is and presto, he is on Auto-teach or Robo-learn. Well, in my humble opinion, that is not the way it works. Such a plan might be contraindicated. Students already spend too much time staring into computer screens. (You know for facebook, twitter and video games). This fouls up their vision as listening to loud rap music fouls up their hearing. So, when the teacher pulls down a map and shows them the location of Mexico, they can't see the map, and they think she said, "This is where the Jews celebrate their annual feast of Holocaust."

No single factor is screwing up our educational process. To quote scripture, "A lot of little foxes that spoil the vines" (Song of Solomon 2:15) Teachers are the politicians' favorite scapegoats. A few bad apples are terrible at their job and would be better suited selling Avon, Accords, or even acorns, since they are themselves nuts. Nevertheless, the vast majorities are sincere dedicated people who have spent a lot of time and money preparing to teach. They wind up getting paid a lot less than some of their students who sell marijuana. Speaking from actual experience, I think that teachers are overburdened today with paperwork to the point that they do not have time to teach. They have to prepare lesson plans before they teach, post them on line so parents will know what little Johnny is supposed to be doing, teach an over-crowded roomful of kids whose IQ's and learning disabilities vary all across the spectrum. Then they have to document what they have taught after the fact to make sure some bozo can't sue them for dereliction of duty. Teachers are also loaded down with various out of the classroom supervision duties that should be taken care of by over-paid administrators.

Maybe common sense would advise us if we are to solve some of these problems that challenge the educational process, we must first of all come up with a plan to better prepare our teachers before we give them a job. We must weed out the insincere, the uncommitted, and the weak of heart before we give them a teaching certificate. Once certified under our more rigid system, we must give them a comfortable environment designed for maximum learning, the books and accessories required to make it in our high-tech world, a class size that is manageable, and pay them a decent salary so that they don't have to "moon-light" at Wally World in order to pay their rent. Oh, I almost forgot. We must not neglect fair and proper supervision. We must send highly qualified, unbiased instructional leaders into their classrooms on a regular basis to make sure that teachers are teaching. Do not assign this important task of teacher evaluation to an ex-coach who is now an assistant superintendent who got his job because he was well liked by the school board or was the winningest coach ever to grace the sideline unless he is also a certified, bona-fide, and qualified instructional leader.

One very real factor in the educational process that I have not mentioned is parents. Do they really have any impact on what junior makes on his graduate exam? You better believe it! Aside from those little bits of genetic information that Watson and Crick called DNA, they pass on a lot to their children. In other words, the nut does not fall far from the tree. Parents, before you launch a Blitzkrieg attack against the school board, teachers, and administrators for junior's failure to learn, ask yourself a few questions. Have I been a good example and role model in the learning process? Have I been available to assist junior with his homework? Did I read to him before he could read for himself? Did I encourage reading by taking him to a library or buy him books? Did I praise him every time he made an academic accomplishment even if it were only a smiley face and not a first place ribbon? Did I explain to him the importance of getting an education in today's society? Have I provided the best possible home learning environment? Have I practiced "tough love" and insisted that Junior put away the video game and facebook so that he could devote quality time to his studies? Education of our children is a team effort, and parents are a vital part of that team. Parents must never minimize their role in the educational process. More often than not, parents are unfortunately part of the problem rather than an asset to the process and accomplishment of the goals of education. Having to deal with absentee, irate, ignorant, apathetic and sometimes hostile parents can make teaching a very challenging occupation.

Parents, if you are lucky enough to have some good teachers at your school, thank them for dedicating their lives to your child. Ask them if they need anything in the way of instructional supplies that you or a group of likeminded parents can provide. Let them know you are in their corner ready to assist in whatever way that would make a positive contribution to the educational process. Why? Because they are "in loco parentis." They are you when you aren't there. They are taking over the raising of your baby. They are there to help that baby learn, grow, and develop. Those teachers are largely responsible for preparing your child to make a living in the cruel and competitive world where few jobs exist. Your baby's teachers will be largely responsible for how he, or she, interprets the world, how he, or she, feels about himself, or herself, others, and the government of our country. Let them know that you expect and demand that they give their best effort in educating your child. They must be sure to plant seeds of confidence, enthusiasm, and optimism within their hearts. Challenge them to ensure your child believes that anything is possible, that no doors are closed that can't be opened, and that no dreams are too impossible to achieve. Remind them that you are entrusting your most valuable possession to their care. Then thank them and support the school with your presence at all events and functions.

The position and priority of education in our national budget may also deserve close scrutiny to ascertain whether the reservoir of common sense might be low here as well. I am sure education is in the budget. I am just not sure where it falls in priority. I would guess from merely looking at the terrible condition that many of our schools are in that its place in the budget is very near the bottom scrunched between national park rest room maintenance and grants for researching why turds stink and why vultures are bald. (I will actually address this issue elsewhere in this book.) The teachers into whose hands we entrust our children receive an average salary of $41,351.00. The average salary for a congressman is at least three times that amount. Is it any wonder why so few choose teaching for a vocation, and why we have a serious shortage of well-qualified teachers today? The shortage is so serious that we have to recruit teachers from other countries. We get most of our goods from China—why not our teachers? Apparently principals are also scarce at times. One year in our not so distant past at least 160 schools in America started the school year without a principal. That is like starting a sumo wrestling match or a college football game without officials. Someone is gonna need a band-aid. Maybe in some of the cases, it was an experiment to prove one of Newton's Laws. Is there really a reaction for every action? Or maybe it was an experiment to verify one of the theories of how the universe began. Can order come spontaneously out of chaos?

Why can't a country like ours with so many millionaires, billionaires, and almost millionaires, scrape up enough money to pay our teachers a decent salary and provide a safe and effective learning environment for our students? Shamefully, students have to get out on the street and sell donuts to raise money to buy lab equipment. Fund raisers are fine, in their place. In fact some, like the ones we used to have at New Hope Junior High in north Coffee County, Alabama, were good morale builders for the school and community. At our annual barbeque, all the men on the faculty, along with some fine volunteers from the community, would pitch in and do all the work necessary for a successful BBQ. We had a ball sitting around the outdoor cooking pit, turning the meat when required, adding coals, and adding the salt and vinegar in the final stage of the cooking process. We would stay up all night working in shifts and catching up on all the interesting gossip which wasn't much. We men cannot find nearly as much juicy gossip as our female counterparts. That may be because women are smarter and more creative in this respect. When there is nothing worthwhile, profound or impressive enough to startle our pals, we will sit in silence for long periods of time until one of us has a fresh inspiration. Women on the other hand, will actually invent stuff to say in order to prevent periods of silence from making the evening a total bore. Anyway, the women and some student volunteers would busy themselves making coleslaw, baked beans, rice, and pound cake to serve along with the B.B.Q. pork. We had a fun time working to keep the community united in common causes. Sometimes we gave part of the money raised to needy families or to fund some special educational program. My point is that such fund-raisers should always be for extras and should not be necessary to provide the basic needs of the educational process.

Because of insufficient funding, many of the schools in America are literally falling in or falling apart. As recently as 1999, twenty-five percent of the school systems in America reported that they had inadequate buildings. Teachers are holding classes across America in mobile classroom units, halls, gyms, cafeterias, and even outside. In addition, nearly eleven percent of schools in the U.S. have enrollments that are more than twenty- four percent greater than the capacity of the physical plant. Ironic as it may seem, the same congressmen who refuse to fund education adequately to eliminate these and other problems are the same ones who pee in their pants and pitch a fit because our kids are so far behind the kids in other developed countries. These same congressmen cry out for "accountability" so they push for teacher testing and more and more student testing. Teachers spend so much time

testing now that they don't have time to cover the required curricula.
I bet that a lot of teachers would like to administer a standardized test
to congress. I recall a joke in which that actually happened. A senate
sub-committee was given an I.O. test and the results were negative!
O.K. Maybe it wasn't a joke.

Another major problem confronting education is the high drop-
out rate. Thirty three percent of our students are dropping out of high
school. This means that every day almost 7,000 students leave school.
The casualty rate is even greater for minorities who have about a forty
nine percent drop-out rate. Statistics confirm that drop-outs are more
likely to get hooked on drugs and commit crimes than students who
stay in school. Convictions usually result in jail time. Who pays for the
room and board of these drop-outs turned criminals? You got it. We,
the people, do. So when education fails and large numbers of drop-outs
turn to crime, society picks up the tab. The drop-out rate for colleges
is not much better. Over one third of students entering community
colleges drop out before getting diplomas. The main reason we are
told, is lack of adequate preparation. They are simply not prepared to
be successful even in the basic college courses. Not only do ill-prepared
high school graduates find out that they can't make it in college, many
are finding out that they cannot get jobs or hold jobs in America's
workplace. Again, the reason is poor preparation. Albeit, the eggheads
in the top echelons of academia have come up with a brilliant solution.
They used the LTS approach. (Lower The Standards). Since so many
high-school seniors were failing graduate exams, the people calling the
shots saw a quick fix—Make the test easier.

Nick Saban is probably the best college football coach in America
today. Since taking over at the University of Alabama, he has already
won three national championships. What is the secret of his success? I
don't know the complete formula, but I can assure you of this. He did
not lower any standards. I think the main ingredients in his success
recipe are hard work and preparation. He prepares his players for tough
games by subjecting them to even tougher practices. If the practices
are more physically demanding than the games, players who wear
the crimson and white feel as if the Saturday game is a walk in the
park compared to the daily grueling practices. The players are drilled

in situation response. They will not be confronted in a game by any situation that they have not been exposed to many times in practice. If our educators would adopt this philosophy for our schools, I am confident that we would start turning out graduates ready for college and ready to perform admirably in the workplaces of America. They would at least be competent in reading comprehension and math which would prepare them for reading rental leases, insurance policies, bank statements, credit terms, and other documents which the average person has to face in our society. The federal government has too much control of how high the standards are set for our students. If these low standards are the cause of our disappointing performance in education when compared to other developed countries, the common sense solution is like the solution to so many of our other problems. **Return to the Constitution**. According to this document, education was never intended to be a function of the federal government. Let each state determine the educational needs, set policy, experiment with merit pay vs. tenure and try other "out of the box" strategies. Who knows, someone or some group of exceptional teachers might come up with a great plan that works.

Before leaving the subject of education we must address the issue of what, if anything in addition to the three Rs, should be taught in our public schools? I think most high schools teach history classes. Hopefully, these classes include a little patriotism and love of country. If students know where they came from as a nation, it will be easier for them to see where they are headed in the future. History must have lost its significance as a required college course in at least three institutions. A student can get a degree at Harvard, Yale, and Stanford without taking a single history course. Remember. I have already stated, "A nation that does not learn from its mistakes is destined to repeat them."

Science and math courses must be taught, and taught well in our high-tech society. Students in several other nations are now ahead of the United States in these two vital subjects. These are difficult subjects. Teachers in our elementary schools must be creative in their methods in order to stimulate interest and enthusiasm in these endeavors.

Three other subjects that I consider vital for all schools are drama, art, and music. I have learned from personal experience what can happen if competent instructors teach these subjects. When I taught biology and coached basketball at Zion Chapel High School in rural Coffee County, Alabama, I directed a three-act comedy. For years, no kind of drama had been presented at that school. In fact the stage had been demolished at some point. No one told me to do this. Directing a play was not part of my contract. I received no pay for this endeavor. However, I realized that we had many talented kids whose interests and talents did not include football, basketball, or baseball. No, directing a play was not easy. We had to build a portable stage in the gym. Next, we had to retrieve some stage curtains from a closed junior high school and install them in the high school gym. We held practices before and after school. All the hard work and preparation paid huge dividends. On the night of the performance, drama instructors from three in-state colleges were in attendance. When all the dust had settled and the final curtain had closed, three grateful seniors received full scholarships in drama to various institutions. I feel strongly that every state should be required to offer these subjects as part of the regular curriculum. Studies done by the Education Commission of the States, with findings not surprising and not contradictory to what I already knew, reported; "There is a strong correlation between art and music education and lower high school drop-out rates." Offering these subjects helps turn a boring, clockwatching uninteresting day into a meaningful experience for those students who would otherwise drop out. In art, drama, and music classes they can feel equal to peers, experience real success, and look forward to coming to class the next day.

Finally, let's talk about manners and morals. Is it sensible to include these items in the curriculum taught in our schools? Teddy Roosevelt might not have been an experienced instructional leader, but he did know how to teach. Just ask those Cubans that he stormed past as he ascended San Juan Hill. On this subject Roosevelt stated, "To educate a man in mind and not in morals is to educate a menace to society." I also like Plato's common sense thought about education, "By education I mean that training in excellence from youth upward which makes a man passionately desire to be a perfect citizen and teaches him to rule and to obey with justice. This is the only education which deserves the name. That other sort of training which aims at acquiring wealth or bodily strength is not worthy to be called education at all." The mind must be stimulated and challenged; the body must be strengthened and invigorated so that biological functions including the working of the brain will be at their best. Most significantly, we must not forget that the heart of education is the education of the heart. It has been said that America is great because she is good and when we cease to be good, we will cease to be great. We cannot have the harvest of greatness when we cease to sow the seeds of goodness. Therefore, we must teach the seeds of goodness to our children. How can we teach them the history of our great nation without teaching them the God of this history? All our founding fathers did not share the same belief about God, but one thing is for sure. They were smart enough not to leave Him out completely. We must not listen to the absurd atheists and let a minority of unbelievers dictate to the majority what we can say and teach about God in our schools.

At the conclusion of every lesson, good educators usually give a quiz. This seems like a good time and place for me to give you, the reader, a simple and short fill-in-the blank quiz. In the course of this book I have given you information about the meaning of words and about how our government does or does not work. Therefore, you should not have much difficulty in making a good score on this test. It consists of only one question:

1. If pro is the opposite of con then the opposite of progress must be _____. (hint—the answer also refers to a herd of baboons) Please note that the answer to this question might also explain, to a large degree, why we still have so many problems with education in America.

Education, like government, will not be improved until we, the people, demand improvement. Education will improve in America when we improve the preparation and pay for our educators, improve educational physical plants, re-establish academics as a priority over sports, and return common-sense, morals, prayer, and Bible reading to our schools.

CHAPTER VII

THE FEDERAL GOVERNMENT MUST BE REPRESSED AND REDUCED

When I was a youngster growing up and learning about the world, I would often get in over my head, or get into various and sundry mischief. I wanted to be good and do right, but there were just too many other options. Very often my mother or teacher, upon learning of my most recent episode of misbehavior, would shake a finger at me and exclaim, "Young man, you are getting too big for your britches." I didn't know the origin of that expression but I knew the meaning. Simply, I had overstepped my bounds, got out of line, missed the mark, broken some rule, or sinned against the Holy Ghost. I often found myself on the wrong side of the law for committing what I considered minor stuff, like poking whatever food I didn't like down the hollow aluminum legs of our kitchen table. I'm a boomer, and as you probably already know, most baby-boomers are the children of parents who went through the depression. We didn't waste anything at my house, especially food. I sincerely wish that all of our elected officials, who are in charge of our tax dollars, could go back in time and live at my house for a month. They would learn how to economize and stop wasting.

I am convinced that much waste in our government results from not only a lack of common sense, but also because our government has become "too big for its britches." Our government leaders are guilty of committing all the atrocities that I committed as I was growing up in those "too big britches."

Our government is not only too big for its britches, but it has too many wrinkles. Yes, that aptly describes our government, "too big for its britches" and "too many wrinkles." Two old ladies were sitting in their rockers on the front porch of the local nursing home discussing how women are not really from Venus, men are not really from Mars, and how rude and red-neck Michelle Obama acted when she applauded for the lies her husband was telling during the 2012 town hall presidential debate. Both ladies were enjoying a dip of snuff, when out of nowhere a totally naked eighty-five year old man came around the corner "streaking." Maybe he was not streaking in the true sense of the word because his top speed was only two miles per hour. He was moving slowly enough so that the ladies could get a really good look at every aspect of his anatomy. Had they been artists with pen and paper in hand, they could have drawn him accurately enough for the police to find him. One of the senior ladies swallowed her snuff and was rendered speechless, but the other managed to ask, "What was that, Maude?" Finally recovering from eating a cud of ground tobacco, Maude replied, "I don't know but it sure did need ironing"

Too big, too slow, too many wrinkles, and needs cleaning and ironing! That aptly describes our government. Many problems are associated with a government that is too big for its britches. I will mention only two at the present: First, the larger the government, the more power it assumes. Second, the larger the government, the less accountability it has. In other words, who is responsible for what gets lost in one of the wrinkles? A government that is too big for its britches is a disaster for the people. A severe drought in Texas, a wildfire in California, a tornado in Alabama, and a flood in Louisiana—what do all these have in common? Very soon after these events occur, the newsman will appear on T.V. and announce, "The president has declared this state or county to be a disaster area." Federal aid is rushed to the scene. When will Washington D.C. be declared a disaster area? Obviously, government leaders will never declare themselves a disaster area because they are too busy voting themselves salary increases. We, the people, must do it. We taxpayers must make a declaration of disaster of our own. The first thing we could do is have some huge signs painted and placed on every road leading into D.C. that read, "Caution, now entering a disaster zone." Surely some of our elected officials would get the message.

We have seen so much stupidity flow out of Washington's disaster zone that we must change our quest in America from a search for the "fountain of youth" to a search for the "fountain of smart." Momma taught me that I should always try to say something nice about folks. Well, the nicest and most positive thing that I can truthfully say about that place is "If you don't count the killings, Washington D.C. has a very low crime rate." If you think I am being too hard on our policy makers, consider all the crises threatening our country. Yet, our so called statesmen recently spent hours debating the topic of "what should be America's official language?" I am not kidding! They finally agreed that it is English. Bright boys, aren't they? Give'em a raise. No don't bother! They will take care of that matter of business next session.

Our government has become a jugger-naught, a King Kong, out of control, brainless behemoth. Under the direction of chief ogre, Obama, more evil plagues have been unleashed on our country than Moses turned loose on Pharaoh and the Egyptians. He doesn't bother with consent of the people. Heck, he does not consult with congress before he defecates on America. (That is not the word I would have used as a bootlegger's son.) Since that time I have become refined and cultured. Besides, I may be writing to some genteel southern ladies who would blush at the language of my youth. I am reminded of what Barry Goldwater said about an overweight government on steroids, "A government big enough to give you everything you want is also big enough to take away everything you have." Our founding fathers tried to idiot-proof our system of government, but the American gene pool keeps sending better and better idiots to D.C.

Let me show you an example of how politicians work. I am a Chevrolet man and always have been. Yet, if I'm afoot and need a ride, I will ride in a Ford. However, I will take a hot, soapy bath, as soon as possible, after riding in a Ford. Now, if I am debating cars and Chevrolet happens to have a bad year (I admit we did have one dismal year—the year we made the Corvair), and I can't come up with anything to promote Chevrolet, my natural tactic, as a politician, is to bad-mouth Ford. So, I launch into the Acronyms for F.O.R.D.- Found On Road Dead, and Fix Or Repair Daily. Then I will lambast their founder and CEO. Americans, I'll bet you didn't know that Henry Ford did not invent the automobile—Gottlieb Daimler and Karl Benz of Germany and Charles Duryea of the U.S. did. Ford only refined them. Neither did Ford introduce the assembly line to auto manufacturing. Ransom E. Olds did, in 1901, increasing his factory's output of Oldsmobiles from 425 cars that year to 2,500 the next. Ford simply improved on the idea by speeding up production of the model "T" from a day and a half to an hour and a half to build one of the Tin Lizzies. Now, what has all this to do with politics and our congress?

We, as taxpayers, have to ride, drive and live with what comes out of Washington, along with paying the price tag. Given these facts, we want them to deliberate carefully, think clearly, and vote wisely. We want them to be efficient and careful about how they spend our tax dollars, but we do not want them to rush important legislation through the process like Ford did the Model T. Problems and recalls are inevitable if cars and bills are rushed through too quickly. Cars need to be inspected. Bills need to be read, understood, and deported of sly add-on subterfuges. We cannot allow passage of a thousand page tax document to be passed in panic, often without being read or understood by the majority of the law-makers. This clandestine, crooked, and irresponsible practice must be stopped. Some of their incompetent, incomprehensible management of our money and freedoms goes beyond defying common sense. It defies sanity. If one of our aged parents begins overspending and mismanaging their bank accounts to the verge of bankruptcy, what would we do? We would take aggressive action to help. We would acquire power of attorney and take control. We must do the same with our politicians before they bankrupt our great country. We must act now. We must not sit silently in the shade sipping sarsaparilla. We cannot let the drunken sailors in Washington plot a course that will certainly lead our children and grandchildren to shipwreck and peril beyond recovery. The tyranny and treachery in America has grown to the proportion of a tyrannosaurus. This tyranny, like the massive dinosaur is carnivorous and will gobble us up.

We Americans have become weak and anemic like a barefoot poverty stricken lad whose intestinal tract is infested with parasites; only in our case, the blood suckers are on the outside of our bodies. I recall the words of one of my neighbors, a plain-spoken red neck, who nevertheless sat on the city council of a nearby town. When called to testify before a state judge, he let his anger and lack of tact get the better of him. When the judge rubbed him the wrong way, overruling an objection made by the city's attorney, he had these words to say, (I will not use his actual words on this quote, lest you genteel southern ladies faint, and therefore not be able to finish this glorious book.) "Your honor, I'm just a red-neck country hayseed, and I know I've got bull butter on my boots, (for you city folks, bull butter is that black, smelly substance found in piles all over cow pastures) but in your case, the bull butter ain't on the outside." This was not a very tactful thing to say to a judge during a serious trial; nevertheless, I do admire his spunk and eloquence. What he says does in fact aptly describe not only many of our federal judges, but a whole lot of our representatives sent to D.C. to protect out liberties and secure our freedoms. Many of the messes they create make us quickly don our waders because we don't know how deep the bull-butter will be that is heaped upon us.

Politicians have become masters of the C.C. Strategy; What is the C.C. Strategy? If you can't convince them, confuse them. We have a nation filled with confused people today. Apparently the majority of Americans that voted in the last presidential election are so confused that they prefer socialism to capitalism. They would forfeit their freedoms and liberties for a free meal. They would rather have a free Obama Phone than freedom of speech. Many have been blindly led into a class war in which those who are too lazy to work, think the rich ought to support them. When a little common-sense is applied to this scenario, it becomes clear, sooner or later, everyone will quit working if the government continues to take larger and larger chunks out of their pay-checks. It is an easy sell for politicians to confuse the working class into thinking that only the rich should be and will be taxed. As I have already stated in chapter four, the hated income tax began as a tax that applied to the wealthiest one percent of Americans. This tax spread like a flu virus until everyone felt the cruel burden of this wretched tax.

We can no longer tolerate the pillaging of our paychecks, the looting of our liberties, and the reckless wasting of our resources. The form of government that we have allowed to develop and evolve in our country today is a misshapen mutation that looks no more like what our founding fathers laid out than a teddy bear looks like a toolbox. Our government has proven to be an uncontrollable, unreliable, and unaccountable entity in preserving "life, liberty, and the pursuit of happiness." Our leaders continuously get us into financial pickles by overspending and misspending our tax dollars. They are like a couple who live down the road from me. He will spend twenty dollars on an item worth ten dollars, if he thinks he needs it, and she will spend ten dollars for something worth twenty dollars, if it is on sale, whether she needs it or not.

Maybe the enemy is we the people. Too often we spend money we don't have to buy things we don't need in order to impress people we don't like. The last part of this statement changes in the case of our politicians; they try to impress people whom they want to vote for them for favors rendered. Spock would say, "Captain, it is not logical for you earthlings to try to fix a debt crisis with more spending." "Thank you, Mr. Spock." "We want you to run for senate in our district after you wipe out the Klingons." If only Mr. Spock could bottle his Vulcan logic. Maybe we could let all our school children have a nation-wide donut sale and raise enough money to buy barrels of it. We could then store it in Fort Knox in the space where our gold used to be. Our congressmen could then make daily withdrawals.

Thomas Jefferson had something to say about dooming our posterity to the bonds of debt: "Politicians are unauthorized to saddle posterity with our debts and morally bound to pay them ourselves." Bernie Madoff did, in the private sector, exactly what Thomas Jefferson warned our government leaders not to do, and we put him in jail. Let common sense be resurrected and applied to our justice system. Let's cry out for justice to be meted out equally and fairly. Let's give our ponzi-pushing politicians some prison privation and see if it deters future pilfering of our posterity's privilege to be debt free. The Ponzi schemes made legal by our legislators, who consider themselves above the law, are not only financially irresponsible, but in fact, blatant acts of criminal negligence. I actually tried to calculate our grandchildren's unsecured debt on a small calculator that I purchased from Wal-Mart. (Any Wal-Mart executives reading this, please take note that I do make a lot of purchases from you guys, and I will be eternally grateful for all that you buy from me.) I punched in the numbers for Social Security, medicare, national debt, interest on debt, cost of present wars, cost of any future wars that Obama might engage in without consulting congress, and the estimated cost of a war with Iran (which is probably inevitable). As I paused to rest my fingers from an exhaustive workout and think of any expenses I might have omitted, the little calculator started smoking, beeping, and flashing its L.E.D. Then it faded into calculator heaven. I reckon I overloaded the little device. Not to worry though, I will take it to the service department of the nearest Wal-Mart, tell them it was defective, and get a new one.

Our congress today is like a Kaleidoscope of fragmented colors, each struggling for expression. What we need is a rainbow of organized, unified colors that don't clash. We Americans need something real, practical, and born of common sense on which we can depend. We need to see red, white, and blue, not only waving in the wind, but engraved and embedded in the hearts of our leaders. I'm afraid that when many of our politicians sing, "America the Beautiful," the sound comes from their diaphragm and not from their hearts. A very astute news reporter wrote the following headlines while covering a coal-miners' strike, "If the strike isn't settled quickly, it may last awhile." He must have been an out-of-work congressman. (I wonder if he got a Pulitzer for the headline alone.) Likewise, if the insanity in D.C. is not cured quickly, it will only get worse, cost more, and drag on for eternity. Talk is cheap except when congress does it. To be fair, we will give them the benefit of the doubt. Maybe most of them are doing what they think their missions are. Maybe they are just confused about what they were sent to D.C. to do. My grandmother used to send me to the store to get two items; invariably, I would be overwhelmed by all the candy and would forget what I was sent to the store to buy. Maybe they are like the police that former Chicago Mayor Richard Daley talked about when he stated, "The police were not there to create disorder; they were there to preserve disorder." Amen, Mayor! This not only applied to your policemen, but aptly describes our congressmen at times. They have done a great job of preserving disorder. According to them, if they get caught with their hand in the cookie jar, "We have not committed a crime. We have just failed to comply with the law."

Talk about forked tongues, I believe they too often have followed Yogi Berra's advice which is, "When you come to a fork in the road, take it." Hey, and all you Republicans, don't be too hard on Joe Biden for telling a man in a wheel chair to stand up. He might have figured that if Obama was Black Jesus, then he must at least be an apostle with the gift of healing. No, forgive him for the faux passe. The rest of the idiots in D.C. are no better. They are telling Americans to "cough up" more money when our pockets are already as empty as if we all went through a gauntlet of Hoover vacuum cleaners. We can no more afford to have more money taken from our paycheck than that poor fellow could stand up. Americans are paying over thirty-nine various and sundry taxes to support an inept and inefficient bureaucracy. On January 1, 2010, over 40,000 new laws and regulations went into effect which will aid and abet the already too powerful and wrinkled government as it seeks to control and fleece the taxpayers of America.

When Coach Paul "Bear" Bryant arrived as the new coach at the University of Alabama, the team had twenty managers. All were fired except one. Bear allowed most of the others to work their way back and earn a place in the program. Let me tell you what I'm thinking here. If we could somehow get "Ole Bear" to take a vacation from his current job as assistant coach of the number one team in Heaven, (God is the Head coach; even Bear has to be accountable to someone) and spend just one session with our boys in D.C., he would first of all, thin out the ranks quick, fast, and in a hurry. I can hear him now as he would have each come into his office one by one and ask, "Why are you here, boy?" Are you here to do the job the people of your district elected you to do, and sincerely try to make the world a better place, or are you here to feather your own nest and see how much money you can make? By the way, have you called your momma today? She might have some advice for you." He would transform them from a bunch a losers into the best legislators the world has ever seen. When Bryant arrived at the capstone, there were one hundred and fifty players on scholarship at Alabama. When they played their first game, only thirty-six dressed out. No doubt, some were loafers with ability but were too lazy to perform. They had to go. The team probably had one or two with no talent who had to be cut even if their dads were rich, influential senators. Some players thought they could play, but in reality, had no ability to play at the college level. Bear would provide them a suitcase and bus ticket. A few players had genuine ability but were un-coachable. They also had to go. Others wanted to break team rules and society's rules thinking they were so good the law did not apply to them. Bear sent them home. In fact, many of these players who were dismissed from Alabama's team might have landed in D.C. They certainly had the right mentality for the job.

Another true story illustrates how our government's size and complexity affects it efficiency. In the seventh chapter of Judges, God chose a fellow named Gideon to deliver the Israelites from the oppression of the vicious and ungodly Midianites. At first, Gideon had an army of 32,000 men. God told him that this was too many. Gideon told the people in Judges 7:3, "Whosoever is fearful and afraid let him return and depart early from Mount Gilead." In other words, "Cowards, get off the battlefield and go home." The next verses tell us 22,000 men were honest enough to admit that they would rather be back in their tents, dining on dates, and chugging camel's milk than slashing about with spears and swords. God told Gideon that the army was still too large. God instructed Gideon to take his men down to the river to drink water, so that they could be further tested to see who was fit for battle. God wanted an elite force of fighting men. He wanted navy seals and green berets. He wanted an Alabama Football team! It is interesting how God made his final selection for the mission of wiping out the Midianites. Those who lapped water like a dog were told to go home. This left only 300 men to accomplish the impossible. We must remember that nothing is impossible with God. God's battle strategy for Gideon was absolutely novel. No army had ever gone into battle before armed with trumpets and clay pitchers containing lighted candles. When you do things God's way, not your way, you can always count on victory, even against overwhelming odds. Judges explains that the combined forces of Midianites, Amalekites, and other hostile nations aligned against Israel that day were so many that they resembled the hordes of grasshoppers which Moses unleashed on Egypt. Also, their camels were too many to count. Listening to God's directions, Gideon and his 300 faithful soldiers completely routed the enemy. I think greatly reducing the size of our government and filling the congressional seats with men of God, who do not lap water like a dog or mess on the ground anywhere they please like a dog or fight like dogs with each other, would give us something positive and helpful out of D.C. Elvis must have been thinking about a politician when he wrote a song about a dog that had never caught a rabbit. Regardless, Elvis was right. If they, like the hound dog of song, can't catch rabbits and put meat on our table, they "ain't" really our friend. I'm afraid the elusive rabbit of good government has eluded some of our "friends" in D.C. I am also reminded of a picture I have seen of a group of dogs sitting at a table playing poker. Somehow that scene brings to mind our lawmakers gambling nonchalantly with our fate. I read recently of an old preacher who was preaching a revival in another state. When he checked into the motel, he noticed a sign that the management had placed on the wall which read, "We will now accept dogs. We have not yet admitted dogs, but we can have dogs stay here now. After all, no dog ever set the place on fire with a cigarette. No dog ever went out without paying his bill, and no dog ever stole our blankets and towels." Then it had a little notice underneath which read, "If you can get your dog to vouch for you, we'll let YOU stay here too." Here is the acid test for letting our lawmakers stay in office. If their dogs will vouch for them and "Bear" will give them permission to dress out, they can stay in office.

Before leaving the subject of football/politics and how they relate to each other, I must elaborate a little further on our failure to use common sense in our selection of staff members and the tasks we assign them. We often assign members of the coaching staff where they don't belong because of lack of experience or lack of qualifications. We do the same thing by sending unqualified ambassadors to represent us on "the Hill." I had an assistant coach one time whom I asked to get the field ready for Friday night's game. I even went to the football field with him, showed him how to use the 10 yard chains to measure off the yardage on both sides of the field, and then pull a string across the field before painting the lines. This old boy, just like many of our legislators, wanted to take shortcuts, wave the rules, and do it his way. He did use the chains on one side of the field to establish the ten yard increments but decided to "eyeball', or estimate the yard lines on the other side. He pulled the strings and rather than use paint to mark the lines, decided to use diesel fuel to make permanent lines that would last the whole season. I think you already have a mental image of what that football field looked like. We had lines running from a ten yard increment to a seven yard increment in some places and ten yards to twelve yards in others. Needless to say, my principal was furious. He blamed me and asked me why I did not take my biology class with me to the football field and do the job myself, using my biology students as helpers. You have to remember, in the South, football is more important than biology. Listen, some of the crooked lines our congressmen paint do permanent damage to our playing fields as well. If you don't think those boys in D.C. can chalk crooked lines when it suits their purposes, just look at some of their "Gerrymandered" congressional districts. We have to be careful who gets access to diesel fuel.

Our policy makers become disoriented from time to time I reckon and forget where they are and why they are there. I know Ted Kennedy must have been disoriented when he drove his car into the bay. George W. Bush was disoriented the whole time he was in office. Reminds me of another incident involving one of my best friends and fellow coaches, who, like me, has never played a down of football. I have to honor Mike here by giving his real name. I want Mike to know how much I truly appreciate all the things he has done for me over the years not the least of which was to take my family and me into his home and give us a place to stay when our house burned to the ground in December of 1985. We were both coaching at the same high school where another of my best friends David Collins, was the head football coach. David is a great football coach and a wonderful Christian. I am sure he had to question God on many occasions as to why He had sent him two basketball coaches to help run his football program. Coach Collins was very patient with us throughout our learning experience. Both Mike Lindsey and I learned a lot of football from David, and we tried to reciprocate the sharing of sports knowledge. Somehow, in spite of our best efforts, David never learned how to dribble. Mike is a great basketball coach and a dedicated Christian. In our first year of coaching, we had a home game and the guy who usually ran the P.A. system did not show up. Coach Collins, realizing that he would probably be better off if he could get Mike and me off the sidelines and out of his way, seized the opportunity. He suggested that we go to the press box and announce the game. We agreed and off we went. At some exciting point during the game, Mike was telling the spectators the field position of our team. The words will never leave my mind until the day I die, "The Rebels are on the fifty-third yard line, and Robert has dropped back to pass." Don't worry Mike, I have made much larger mistakes than that during my coaching career. (I love you guys. Read this book. Buy two copies for your friends, and tell everybody you know where they can buy one.) Sadly, many of our guys at D.C. are on the fifty-third yard line and they don't know which way to run with the ball.

Our nation has twice as many conservative Americans as Liberals. Whether that is fact or fiction will become apparent on November 6. I suspect, however, that some of the conservatives are only ideologically conservative as opposed to actual conservatives. They may talk like Jefferson and vote like Hamilton. If so, we will know that their commitment to limited government is only hypocritical. We have experienced a mutilation of word meanings over the years. "Liberal" before the F.D.R. era described policies pushing liberty and individual rights. Roosevelt, however, changed it somewhat to mean "collective rights" and "group entitlements." Jay Cost has dubbed it "clientelism." This practice, whatever we call it, has spoiled the once proud Democratic Party and reduced it to a servant of the strong. Please note carefully this next statement.

This type of liberalism, pioneered by F.D.R., develops policies not just to buy the allegiance of existing groups, but to **create** groups that from this point forward would be dependent on government. Roosevelt's plan, which worked better than any of "Bear Bryant's" wishbone plays, was to create an electoral majority from a myriad of client groups. Why do you think teacher unions love democrats? Why do farmers like either party if they pay them when their crops fail? Why do business people like democrats? Tariff protection, maybe. Why do senior citizens like democrats? Pensions, maybe. You get my point. I hope. Government no longer exists to protect natural rights but to grant rights! This isn't right. So, let's change it! All these freebies to any group that would band together to suckle the government teat is bad enough but it gets worse. In 1982, amendments to the Voting Rights Act allowed a few government-approved minorities an "entitlement" to public offices. About forty congressional districts would henceforth be guaranteed to elect minority members. I have considered starting my own grass-roots minority group and demand the Feds give my group our entitlement. My group is going to be called D.A.D.D.D.—Dads Against Daughters Dating Democrats. This group will do a lot of good if we get funded or "entitled". Maybe we can finally stop the democratic perpetual motion machine. We will be like a contraceptive to the perpetuation of democrats. "Yes, dear, you can go out with Rashad even if he is a nose-pierced, long-haired, tattooed, pot-smoking misfit. Just make sure he or his folks are not democrats." Walter Mondale, conceding to Ronald Regan after the 1984 presidential race, listed some groups that he thought ought to be on the government's teat—"the elderly, the poor, the handicapped, the unemployed, and the sad." Yes, if my eyes and ears haven't deceived me, he said "sad."

We once had a "common man" for president in Andrew Jackson. He would have none of this catering to special interest groups rich enough to have lobbyists camp out on the white house steps. He vetoed every piece of legislation that they tried to slide by him. I support Andrew Jackson's thoughts on the subject. He stated, "It is to be regretted that the rich and powerful too often bend the acts of government to their selfish purposes. When government goes beyond equal protection by law and undertakes to distribute wealth and opportunity; the humble members of society—the farmers, mechanics and laborers—who have neither the time nor the means of securing like favors to themselves, have a right to complain of the injustice of their government." Thank God for the tea party—the one in 1776 and the one we have now! They are the only voice crying in the wilderness against such tyranny.

CHAPTER VIII

CONGRESS MUST BE REPRIMANDED AND RESTRAINED

I am a lot like Tony Denozo, very special agent on the NCIS team of sleuths who is always comparing someone or some current situation to a movie he has seen. Apparently he has seen them all because he is never at a loss for a simile or metaphor. One of my favorite movies was "Butch Cassidy and the Sundance Kid" starring Katherine Ross, Paul Newman, and Robert Redford.

In that movie the outlaws Butch and Sundance were relentlessly pursued by a persistent posse that would not give up the chase, even following them so far as South America. On several occasions Butch would ask Sundance, "Who **are** those guys?" They would think they had eluded them and look up to see the dust of their horses once again indicating their proximity to capture. Again the question came, "Who **are** those guys?" They had been fugitives from the law in several states and had robbed a lot of banks and trains, but they had never seen such a determined posse.

In this chapter I will attempt to identify a similar *"posse of elected officials"* whose primary purpose in life seems to be that of tracking down every taxpayer and bleeding him till he is at best anemic and at worst, a corpse. Perhaps the first step in describing our men on the hill is to give them a scientific name. Because of my years of teaching scientific facts about the universe and the flora and fauna that populate our world, I cannot help but wonder at the many similarities between our elected officials and certain animals. Early zoologists, botanists, and taxonomists would try to give appropriate Latin names to our plants and animals based on their physical characteristics and behavior. Knowing the name and some characteristics of an organism before you begin your study makes the study easier. This is the basis of our current discussion.

The Latin name given to organisms usually consists of what we call "binomial nomenclature." In English that means we will give them two names-one for genus and one for species. If you are not gifted in the areas of science, do not misunderstand what I just said. I did not say they would be given a name for their genius-but for genus. A large percentage of our senators and representatives are bald or balding. Ever wonder why? If it has something to do with their kinship to eagles and if they soar like eagles, then we might consider a name that is similar to our American Bald Eagle. I am reminded of one of my favorite scriptures at this point; (Isaiah 40:31) "They that wait upon the Lord shall renew their strength, they shall mount up with wings like eagles…."

I am afraid we cannot put them in a class with eagles. They don't wait on the Lord for an answer before they move forward with legislation. Judging from some of the absurd and illogical legislation that comes from some of their sessions, they must not consult with Him in the first place. I think they should remember what Benjamin Franklin said, "I have lived a long time and the older I get, the more I am convinced that God governs in the affairs of men." Mr. Franklin knew that there should always be one extra seat in congress whose district is the universe and whose constituents are everyone in the world. My mom always told me; "If you hoot with owls at night, you cannot soar with the eagles in the daytime." I'm afraid many of our men on the hill do more "hooting" than "soaring;" therefore, we must not classify them with eagles. Returning to our discussion of baldness, testosterone might be a factor in this singular characteristic of baldness that we are considering but more likely it is their kinship to vultures. vultures are also bald, and they are bald for a very good scientific reason. They are bald in order to stay healthy—That's right—Have you ever seen a sick buzzard? The birds tend to stick their beaks into some very filthy places where all kinds of mites, maggots, and bacteria thrive. Since the buzzards have no feathers on top of their heads, these potentially dangerous life forms have nothing on which to cling. Are you beginning to get my point?

The kinship is eerie, isn't it? Given the excessive number of times some of our elected officials dip into corruption, bribes, kick-backs and other nasty situations, they have to have some means of protection, or they would not live out their terms of office. Therefore, in our naming process we must consider a name similar to the buzzard.

Another scientific name we might consider is one that links them to the groundhog. In view of this term, something like "greedy swine" does have a ring of truth to it. However, groundhogs do not fly, but we know that our elected officials will fly at our expense whenever it is in their best interest. If a large block of votes are at stake, they don't flinch at letting the taxpayers buy them a ticket to any state or foreign country. So "groundhog" might be a misnomer. But when you consider that so many people believe in the myth of groundhogs, we can't rule out this kinship. Be honest now. How many of you somehow suspect that when your senator is talking to you, he is spinning a yarn, pulling your leg or maybe the wool over your eyes. The truth is, groundhogs, including the notorious Punxsutawney Phil, do not come out of their holes in the ground to predict the weather. They come out for two more important reasons—to find food and to chase members of the opposite sex. (Already you are starting to make the association, aren't you?) Perhaps this is why they are wrong in their predictions 72% of the time. (I dare not state the percentage of times our elected officials guess wrong or make false predictions.) Let's not be too critical. Have you ever tried to make accurate weather predictions with three hot female groundhogs in heat hovering around you? Maybe discovering that many of our elected officials have characteristics of vultures and ground hogs, we will have to consider binomial nomenclature that includes both animals.

We must also consider their posture as we attempt to identify them and give them an appropriate name. I once read about two men who almost came to fisticuffs over chickens. They were actually arguing about the English language. One said that it was grammatically correct to say "The hen is setting." The other maintained that it was correct to say, "The hen is sitting." Finally common sense prevailed (Remember. This book is about common sense.), and they agreed to let farmer Brown settle the argument. Farmer Brown, after hearing both sides of the argument, rather contemptuously said, "Men, when I see a hen in such a position on a nest, I don't concern myself with whether she is sitting or setting, I only ask, "Is she **LAYING** or **LYING**?" I don't know if lying is the major problem we have with some of our congressmen or if their *"glibido"* is just too high. A high glibido is easily spotted in a person—all talk and no action.

My oldest grandson, Ayden English is five years old and his favorite pastime is catching any critter that is not big enough to eat him. The other day he had captured a chameleon. "Look what I've got Papa!" "What is it?" I inquired. "I don't know for sure but the way he changes color back and forth, he reminds me of one of those Washington politicians." Yea, I teach my grand boys at an early age about the people, politicians and animals around them. "You are absolutely right. They will not only change color on you midstream, but they sing geographically." "Oh, Papa, you're kidding me now, aren't you?" "No, it's a fact; they will sing "Dixie" with the best southern drawl you ever heard when they are south of the Mason-Dixon Line. Then they will sing "Battle Hymn of the Republic" like a true blue boy from Boston when they are in the North." The song they sing depends on where they are and to whom they are singing.

At this point I related to my inquisitive little entomologist the story of my Uncle Vernon's mule. Every Saturday my Uncle Vernon would knock off plowing at noon and ride the mule he called "Captain Kangroo," Roo, for short, into town to refresh himself and to kill off any extra brain cells that might have accumulated by downing a few Budweisers. When he got to the local beer joint, he remembered that Aunt Spar had told him to pick up five pounds of sugar. He tied his mule to the rearview mirror of what he thought was his friend's truck while he went to fetch the sugar. When he returned to the beer joint, he found that someone had painted old Roo from mane to manure port with green paint. He also noticed that Roo had pulled himself loose from the truck and a rearview mirror was hanging from the lead rope. Uncle Vernon was madder than Archie Bunker when he found out that his daughter was dating a Pollock. He stormed into the joint and screamed, "Which one of you S.O.G.s painted my mule?" (That means "Son of a Gun.") Ya'll thought I was going to cuss, didn't you? That term refers to any person of questionable parentage born amid-ships near a cannon. Uncle Vernon had already rolled up his shirt sleeves and was preparing for a bare knuckle brawl when this guy who looked like a genetically engineered cross between the Hulk and Hercules got in his face and said, "I'm the Rembrandt here. I painted your flop-eared, mangy old mule. Let that be a lesson to you not ever to tie that ugly beast to my truck again. Now what were you going to say?" Crestfallen, Uncle Vernon meekly replied, "I just wanted to let you know that the first coat is dry, and Ole Roo is ready for the second coat." From that day forward we all called the mule "Mr. Green Jeans." Politicians will change their tunes in the face of strong opposition as quickly as my Uncle Vernon did that day. (Please note. A lot of stories circulated about my Uncle Vernon Waldon and Roo. Many were absolutely true; some may have been embellished a tad over the years.) By the way, Uncle Vernon got a new nickname that day as well. From that day on, folks called him "Senator Waldon."

I think I will leave it up to the constituents of each district to assign names to their elected officials. We have absolutely too much name calling, back-stabbing, and mud-slinging as it is. However, before I leave the subject, I will point out that no matter what you call them, if we could get them to work together for a common purpose and the good of all Americans, we would all be so much better off. If we could get them to fly like geese, they would be so much more efficient at the job we hire them to do. Geese, as you no doubt know, fly in a V-formation. Birds don't fly in this manner to keep from losing members or to present a daunting figure to potential predators as some have speculated. They do it because it helps them stay aloft for long distance trips. The flapping of the lead bird's wings generates an updraft that helps the second row and so on down the line. The lead birds change position frequently which allows them to increase their effective range. Can we teach these ole birds in D.C. to fly together in formation? Can we get them on the same page? Can we unify their hearts toward one purpose which is beneficial for all and detrimental to none?

As we all go through these times that vex men's souls, our leaders assure us that all is well. The budget will be balanced. The national debt will be reduced, and jobs will be created. But, I suspect a wave of similar vibes is passing among us. We all sense that something just isn't right in America. I call this eerie feeling **"Deja Moo."** Deja Moo is the feeling that you've heard this **bull** before. Remember that feeling you have when a virus is about to overcome you, and you start toward the medicine cabinet. In fact, America is about to become unglued. Our mighty fortress of freedom is about to crumble because something is not right. Maybe our nation has a problem with the mortar that holds the structure of our republic together. I know we have veered off the foundation. Paul gives us some very wise advice in I Corinthians 3:10-11. Paul's instructions were in reference to building a church, but the same advice applies to homes and governments. "I have laid the foundation and another buildeth upon it. But let every man take heed how he buildeth upon it. For other foundation can no man lay than that which is laid which is Jesus Christ." Whether you are building, a home, a church, or a government, you better heed the advice of the master-builder and follow his plan, or you will build on a foundation of sand, and your structure will sink or be blown away by the first storm.

During my teen-age years, one of the many jobs that I performed was that of mortar mixer for a brick mason. He was a master of his craft. Not only were his bricks and stones laid in perfect alignment but his walls and foundations were very strong. "The secret to the strength of the walls is in the mortar," he would say. He could look at the mortar or crumble a handful onto his trowel and quickly tell me if anything was wrong with the mixture. Many times he would tell me to add more sand or to add more water or to add more cement. Weaknesses and cracks in the fabric or mortar that holds America together are very evident today. The foundations of America are the Declaration of Independence and the Constitution. A close inspection of these documents will show that they are well-constructed. The great men who laid the foundations for these documents used the right mixture. They indeed produced two masterpieces. The future of our great country is shaky and uncertain today because Obama and his socialistic cronies are chewing away at the foundation of America like a swarm of termites. Go see the movie 2016. You will see exactly where Obama wants to take America. Paul says that we must build on the foundation "gold, silver and precious stone."

Obama would have us build with wood, hay, and stubble. He rejects and ignores the Constitution which is the chief cornerstone of America.

We have just seen the tip of the iceberg. Conditions are going to get a lot worse in America. I am not a pessimist—I am a realist. If we keep electing men like Obama as president, the great depression of the thirties is going to seem like a picnic compared to what's in store for us. Our future looks about as bright as that of a college football coach whose team had just been pounded by Bear Bryant's quick little tough guys. "Bear" Bryant's teams were as good at football as the Mafia is at crime. This particular coach was relaxing in his recliner when one of his grandchildren climbed on his lap and said, "Paw, Paw, would you read me the story of the "Three Bears?" He said with a scowl on his face, "Oh my God, you mean there are **TWO** more of them?" America is beat up and bruised today like a team which has just played The Crimson Tide. Our future looks dismal and scary because we have more **"bears"** awaiting us as well.

The common sense "fix" for Congress is for us to identify the congressional men and women who are ruining our country. We must reprimand and rebuke them for any misdeeds or foul play. Any member of congress proven unworthy of his high office because of corruption or crime, must be removed from office. "We the people" can do this cleansing of our Congress by getting more involved in the affairs of government and voting intelligently at every opportunity. Smokey the Bear cautioned, "Only you can prevent forest fires." Likewise, only we the voters can prevent our country from "going to the dogs."

Accountability on the part of our law-makers and awareness and action on the part of "we the people" will go a long way toward fixing most of the problems in America.

Our political leaders may not be solely responsible for the mindset of many Americans today. However, they are throwing fuel on the fires of irresponsibility and seek to create a state of communistic socialism in our great country. They are convincing many voters that they can have privileges without responsibilities, advantages without adversity, sweetness without sweat, and payday without workday. Too many want the advantages of living in America without sharing the work and responsibilities of being Americans. To build with gold, silver, and precious stones is too expensive. So, like dishonest contractors, many politicians ignore the building code and substitute cheaper materials. I do a lot of sculpting in clay and wood. One thing I have discovered, I cannot carve rotten wood. If America is to remain a great nation, we must return to our roots and honor the foundation on which we were established. The fires of testing are already on the horizon. Soon we will be tested as never before. Can we depend on our current leadership with so many un-American, ungodly, and unpatriotic policies to lead our great nation? Some of our so-called statesmen are trying to carve out a nation. Like a quack surgeon, they are only butchering the America we love because they are using rotten wood and have ignored the chief cornerstone.

CHAPTER IX

BAD PRESIDENTS MUST BE REBUKED AND RETIRED

Who is this masked man who calls himself "Mr. Change?" He is not the Lone Ranger, for he has yet to render any true justice to the American west or east. He is not Zorro because he has not righted any of the wrongs which burden millions of Americans. No, he is not the shining knight in armor that he envisions himself to be, for he has yet to rescue any damsels in distress. Lady Liberty, the most important damsel I know, is definitely in distress and may crumble into the New York harbor if we do not remove him from office.

"Every man, like the moon, has a dark side," said Mark Twain. That is certainly true of our current president. He has more secrets than Victoria. Batman, the caped crusader, kept all his secrets hidden away in the bat cave. Superman, the man of steel, kept his secrets frozen in the arctic "fortress of solitude." I don't know where our current comic superhero keeps his secrets, but we will find them. In this chapter we are going to sneak up on his dark side and expose him like a roll of Kodak film. We are going to drag his darkest secrets out into the sunshine like my momma made us do with the bedding in our house during spring cleaning days.

Come join me now as we board the space shuttle "**Obamanation I.**" Let us go where no man has gone before and the liberal press will not dare to go. As we approach the dark side of this lunar landscape, we will see what slithers in the slimy seas of dirty politics, what creeps in the crevices of the corrupt craters, and what lurks in the laboratory of this present day Dr. Jekyll and Mr. Hyde.

Lincoln was called "The Great Emancipator." Teddy Roosevelt was called "The Rough Rider," Andrew Jackson was known as "Old Hickory." Clinton will always be remembered as "I didn't have sex in the Oval Office president" or maybe "Slick Willie." How will Obama be remembered in the annuals of history? Perhaps he will be called "The Great Pretender" because he only "pretends" to be an American who cares about other Americans. He could be called "The Great Spender" because he has spent more of our tax dollars and borrowed more money abroad, than any other president in the history of our country. The Obama story is a sleazy story with more twists, turns, and shenanigans than a John Grisham novel. He has promised so much and delivered so little. His talk is cheap for one main reason. Supply exceeds demand.

In order to unmask our "super-hero," we must call on the opinions of experts to get a valid and true evaluation of his character. First, let's call Dr. Freud. "Sir, could you help us try to understand what is going on with our CEO?" Freud answers, "Well, it is a complicated case, but as I see it, he is an egotistical, narcissistic, and highly prejudiced individual. He's filled with extreme pride and suffering from delusions of grandeur." Next, let's call Deputy Barney Fife. Barney simply says, "He's a nut!" I must agree. He does remind me a little bit of a mixture of Andy Griffith characters. He seems drunk on his own Kool-Aid like Otis Campbell. Like Ernest T. Bass, he runs around throwing rocks at his predecessors and blames them for all his problems, breaks the rules of our Constitution, and most every other tradition that we hold dear in America. He is also like Gomer Pyle, who marched to the sound of a different drummer. When the rest of his platoon was going right, he was going left, but his momma boasted, "Just look at my boy Gomer. I am so proud of him. Everyone else is going the wrong way except Gomer." Yes, we need to take the Obama machine down to Goober's filling station for a tune-up.

While we are calling people for opinions, let's let the Word of God enlighten us on people with too much arrogance. What people say is of little consequence, but what God says is of eternal significance. Psalms 36:11-12 says, "Let not the foot of pride come against me and let not the hand of the wicked remove me. There are the workers of iniquity fallen;

they are cast down, and shall not be able to rise." In Proverbs 8:13, God says that He hates pride and arrogance. In Proverbs chapter 16, verse 18, we read, "Pride goes before destruction and a haughty spirit before a fall." Obama reminds me of what Charles Churchill said of William Warburton, "He was so proud that should he meet the twelve apostles on the street, he'd turn his nose up at them all, and shove his Savior from the wall."

Jerry Clower, God rest his soul, is unfortunate in that he had something undeniable in common with Mr. Obama. Jerry used to sell fertilizer. Obama still does, (the high potency, organic kind). It would be interesting to hear what Ole' Jerry would have to say about our man at the top. I think I knew Jerry well enough that I can guess what he would say if he were here today, "Yaw done and got yorself in a mess—Yaw done let Obama get up a tree with yaw. Somebody better shake him out cause America has got to have some relief." Amen, Jerry!

To get a true assessment of a man's character, we must hear what those who know him intimately have to say. Edward Klein interviewed a few close associates and friends of Obama who have known him a long time. I think we should review what they had to say. Let us not get our information and base our conclusions on the hearsay of political rivals, but let us get the facts from people who know him best. Richard Epstein, Dean of Law School at the University of Chicago where Obama worked as an instructor said; "I do not see any signs of intellectual curiosity or power in Obama." Epstein added, "Obama saw himself as a serious intellectual, whom he definitely was not." This reminds me of one of our space probes looking for intelligent life on Mars. I'm afraid the space probes will come up as empty as Obama's self-search for intelligence.

I have studied the Obama Health Care package. To me, his health care plan has as much chance of success at fixing America's health dilemma as one of Wiley Coyote's traps has of catching the Road Runner. But to be fair, let's consult with someone who should know all about health care.

Dr. David Scheimer, who was Obama's personal physician for twenty-two years and known to be one of those elite leftist who, we would think, would be in Obama's camp, totally disagreed with

Obama's healthcare program. He said, "I look at his healthcare program, and I can't see how it can work—It has no cost control. The head of the Congressional Budget Office said these words concerning Obamacare, "It's going to be incredibly expensive—And the thing that I really am worried about is, if it is the failure that I think it would be, then, health reform will be set back a long, long time." Well, there you have it. Not only will Obama's plan not work to solve the problem, but, will make the problem worse! We have been going backward long enough! Now we must move forward.

I am not sure why we want to hear from Bill Clinton on this discussion of Obama's suitability to lead this nation. It is sort of like asking Archie Bunker to address the issue of bigotry among White Red-necks. Nevertheless, he is a fellow democrat and would like to see his party remain in control of the White House even if it means that a sailor who couldn't pilot a Huck Finn raft, remain at the helm of our great ship. According to our "no sex in the White House" former president, "Obama doesn't know how to be president. He doesn't know how the world works. He's incompetent." I wonder why Brother Bill was not honest enough to say that in his speech at the 2012 democratic convention. Instead, he made about as many excuses for Obama's poor performance over the previous four years as Obama has made during his campaign speeches. Slick Willie said that our country was in such a mess when Obama took over that even Clinton himself could not have fixed it in four years. I don't know what Nick Saban said to the president during the Crimson Tide's visit to Washington when they recognized Alabama's fourteenth national football championship. Saban should have reminded Obama of the mess that he had inherited four years ago when he became the head football coach at the University of Alabama. Further, Saban could have been very truthful, informing Obama to use honesty and common-sense as he tackled America's problems. The facts are, Saban, unlike Obama, was qualified for his job! Saban obeys the rules of the game and teaches his players to do likewise. Nick Saban will roll up his sleeves, get down in the trenches and demonstrate proper blocking techniques to a freshman recruit. Maybe Mr. Obama should actually pick up one of those shovels that he talks about and demonstrate how to use it—just in case any of those jobs he talks about creating materializes.

Obama might be remembered among other things as the A.W.O. L. president, or after Clint Eastwood's speech at the Republican National Convention, "The Empty Chair President." I know running a successful campaign requires his presence, but so does the job he is already getting paid to do. In my humble opinion, if he would just take care of business and fulfill the oath of office according to constitutional guidelines, people in America would be smart enough to recognize a job well done and applaud him for his efforts. However, he is performing his present job very much like he did his senate job. According to Laura Anderson, Deputy Chief of Staff to the Republican leader of the Senate, "He hardly showed up at all. He did not go to committee meetings. He had no interest in the process of government or in learning the process of being a good senator. He had no interest in government itself. He just wanted to stand on the senate floor and give speeches." Reminds me of an old rooster we had on our farm. He was so old that he was no good what-so-ever at servicing the hens; nevertheless, he liked to get on the tallest fence post and crow. Obama is also very much like an old deacon who was a member of one of my early churches. He did not know much about the Bible, but that did not stop him from misquoting it. He did not know much about the church finances and where the money needed to be spent but that did not prevent him from objecting to every project we planned that involved spending any money. (By the way, he did not tithe.) He did not know much about the true mission of the church and how we wanted to reach everyone regardless of race, creed, or economic status. He once remarked, after a rough looking couple with dirty clothes and uncombed hair were exiting our sanctuary, "Preacher, we don't need them kind of people in our church." Obama's logic on the budget is very much like that of another old deacon about whom I have read. On one occasion a church to which the old gentleman belonged, wanted to buy a chandelier for the church. Of course, the old fellow was "agin" it. When asked why, he had three very good reasons. First, "We ain't got nobody heah that can play it. Second, we ain't even got nobody that can spell it, and Third, We need that money to buy some lights fer the church." If ignorance is bliss—God "Bliss" you, Old fella, and God "Bliss" you, Obama.

Obama, like a lot of people who somehow make it to the top, easily forgets the people who helped him climb the ladder of success. Stephen Rogers is just one of the many people Obama used like a corncob in an outhouse and then threw down the toilet. Mr. Rogers helped raise a lot of money for Obama and other democrats. He did not ask for much in return. Mr. Rogers asked Mr. Obama to return to Northwestern University, where he was a professor, to speak to his students. After he was elected, the students at Northwestern requested that Obama come and speak. He turned a deaf ear to their calls. Finally Mr. Rogers called him to make the request. According to Mr. Rogers, Obama had this to say, "Listen, I can't come. I'm inundated with requests. I have governors calling me. I have Warren Buffet calling me. I have Oprah Winfrey calling me." When asked about the money that Mr. Rogers had given to his campaign, Obama's reply was, "Come on man. You should know better than to believe politicians when they make promises." I wholeheartedly agree with Mr. Roger's final words on the subject of Obama, "What you have with Barack Obama is a lack of character." Well Mr. Rogers, now you know the real definition of a politician like Obama; he is a man so untrustworthy that he will even "double" cross a "bridge" when he comes to it. No, Mr. Rogers, he is not a good president, and he is not a man of his word. He is a good diplomat. Let's fire him as President and appoint him as ambassador to Iran. Then he can tell the Iranians to "go to that dark place of eternal fire where there will be weeping and gnashing of teeth" in such a way that they will look forward to the trip. We have other options of what to do with an unproductive and unpopular president.

The early framers of our Constitution had many challenging questions to debate. One of the hardest issues to decide was how long a president should serve. Madison advocated unlimited terms of office, but others questioned, "Wouldn't that be just like a king?" Franklin replied, "What will you do if you get stuck with a really bad president? The only recourse would be to shoot him." Mr. Franklin, pardon my interruption, but I have a better solution. Exile, yes, banish him to Elba. No, not the island of Elba, where Napoleon was exiled, but the city of

Elba in south Alabama. Yeah, send him there and tell him that he has to make a living for his family under all the policies which he set up while impersonating an American president. Don't feel too bad, Mr. Rogers. He lied to many others as well. Obama told us that he would have us back on our feet in no time with his stimulus package. He was right. Many of my friends had to sell their cars to pay their share of the budget deficit.

A traitor and a con man will use people to achieve their ends. Obama even used the church to further his political agenda. Just ask Reverend Wright, Obama's former pastor. It is a given that businessmen and politicians will use the golf course to boost business and promote political programs. Only a first-class, hypocritical scum-rat will use the church for these purposes. According to Rev. Wright, "Church is not their (Barack and Michelle's) thing. It never was their thing."

When we pull the mask off Obama, what will we find? He seems to hide behind more disguises than Sherlock Holmes on the trail of some evil criminal. He even has David Axelrod, one of his main aides, thinking that he is the Black Jesus. I've got news for you, Mr. Axelrod, He ain't even a close second. Scripture tells us that in the last days, a false Christ would arise. (Matt. 24:5) I think we are there. We are certainly seeing many of the signs.

Have you ever taken your automobile to a mechanic for repair and after leaving it in the shop for a week and paying an ungodly repair bill, drive it out of the garage only to find that it ran worse than before? That is exactly the scenario we have with Mr. Obama. In spite of all his flowery speeches and generous promises, we are no better off. In fact we are worse. As Mr. Obama seeks to implement his programs, he constantly speaks of bumps in the road. Well, my friend, we Americans have been traveling on the Obama turnpike for over four years, and we have indeed encountered more bumps than a bedbug crawling over Dolly Parton. Actually, his bumps have been more like avalanches and gullies of Grand Canyon proportion. He is a shade-tree mechanic at best and apparently does not know a screwdriver from a torque wrench. His $868 billion dollar stimulus program worked about as well as the Hindenburg. Because of Obama's malpractice and ineptitude, the American people are in the position of the old woman mentioned in the Bible who had spent all her money on quacks and rip-off physicians. She discovered she was no better than when she began to seek a cure for her malady. (Luke 8:43)

We must demand and get accountability from our leaders, especially our president. So far, Obama has not been accountable to anyone.

When I was a lad, picking cotton was my only means of acquiring money for school clothes. If I did not pick my quota of cotton every day, Momma would chase me down in that hot dusty cotton field and use a cotton stalk for a purpose for which it was never intended. She equaled George Washington Carver in her creativity in the use of God's plants. She was also very quick and adept at wielding a peach tree switch when my report card was less than satisfactory. Satisfactory for Momma had to be a "B" or better. Fellow Americans, you can grade Obama by anyone's standards and find that he has not made the grade. His cotton sack is more empty than full. His planting borrowed money into the economy has failed miserably. His plan for economic recovery has been tried before with the same result—no improvement in unemployment but a great increase in debt. FDR tried it in 1939 and called it a "New Deal," but it failed. Japan tried their own version of such reckless spending of borrowed money and almost bankrupted their country. LBJ tried to eradicate poverty with his "Great Society" but guess what? The poverty rate even today is the same as it was forty-five years ago. I think an old fashioned whippin from Momma's peach tree switch is in order for Mr. Obama. At any rate, any top executive or college head coach with Obama's performance record would be given his walking papers. Incredulously, our duped and deluded society has given him four more years to ruin America.

As I listen to Obama's bitter criticism of his political opponents, I recall what Paul Harvey said of such criticisms, "You can't make a small man tall by cutting off the legs of a giant." Our man in charge has tried, but his effort to make himself larger, has only shown how small he really is. I think even the majority of blacks in America are beginning to see him for what he is. The only things that have grown about Obama are his nose and right arm. His nose has grown like Pinocchio's, and for the same reason. His right arm is now two inches longer from patting himself on the back for his imaginary accomplishments.

Are we too blind to see that those who do not learn from the mistakes of history are doomed to repeat them? An old Amish proverb reads, "We are too soon oldt and too late schmart." When you discover that you are in a hole, the first step to getting out of the hole is to stop digging. Unfortunately, Obama does not think that way. He has a shovel in both hands. He keeps on digging. He has lied about the thousands of "shovel-ready" projects that were on the horizon in America. These quick-fix projects were supposed to create thousands of jobs. I think we have all learned to turn a deaf ear to a man who has never had to dig with a real shovel. When Obama starts talking about a shovel, as quickly as possible, we must pull on our high top boots because we don't know how deep the poop is going to get. When will he learn the fundamental law of economics? "When the outgo exceeds the income, the upkeep is in for a downfall."

Obama is trying to play a game with rules which he does not understand or bother to learn. Film director Spike Lee said that Obama was a seismic change in the universe and everything in the universe was going to be affected." Of course, that misguided Hollywood hollow head was referring to the Messianic attributes that some have ascribed to Obama. In actuality, the old boy may not be too far off base. A seismic change usually indicates a disaster and is measured on the Richter scale. I give Obama's disaster a perfect 10. After all, in four short years he has managed to mess up more things in America than all the San Francisco earthquakes and coastal hurricanes put together. When Obama encounters a constitutional rule he does not like, he merely ignores it or by political voo-doo, by-passes it. Obama has proven many times "figures don't lie, but liars do figure."

During my school days when my report card was not up to par, I learned the sneaky trick of counterfeiting. Using the same color ink that my teacher had used and being very careful, I could alter my grade and sometimes fool my parents. Obama has forged and counterfeited his report card. He has told us that black is white and white is black and gray doesn't matter. He does not give the American people credit for having enough sense to know when we are being flim-flammed, hoodwinked, and deceived. He thinks he can pee on us and convince us that it is raining. Obama bragged in his 2012 State of the Union

Address about an unemployment rate of eight and one half percent. Compared to the rate of five percent or below during much of the Bush years, this rate is very high. Of course, the Democrats derided Bush for high unemployment.

I would urge all fellow Americans to consider the man without the color. Based on his performance alone, including what he has not done for black Americans, we have no logical reason to even consider this man for president. I truly sympathize for black American voters today. The democratic leaders have taken you for granted thinking you will blindly and thoughtlessly vote democrat all day long. Black voters have been totally ignored by the other party, which thinks there is no reason to bother seeking the black vote. I challenge you to get all the facts from a reliable source. See the movie "2016" to learn about this "Black Jesus" and his destructive agenda for America before you blindly follow him like a herd of lemmings off a cliff. Please realize that he may be a "hounddog," but he "ain't no friend of yours." In fact, one of his problems is trying to run with the rabbits and hunt with the hounds at the same time. Regardless of what Barack Obama tells black Americans when he perches on that fence post and crows, unemployment among blacks reached a twenty-seven year high during his first administration. He claims that he wants a redistribution of wealth and that he wants us all to follow "George Jefferson" and "move on up." He even says he is his brother's keeper. His job of housekeeping and brother keeping has been a dismal failure. The house is still dirty, and the brothers are not any better economically than when Obama first walked into the Oval Office. Understand this fellow Americans, as bad as unemployment is during this administration, it could be worse were it not for demographic factors such as the retirement of so many "baby boomers." Their retirement caused a significant drop in labor force participation, and impacted the rate of unemployment in a positive way.

ALI MIGHT HAVE BEEN THE GREATEST—BUT OBAMA IS NOT THE KING

Obama might just be better at "floating like a butterfly and stinging like a bee" than Ali ever dreamed of being. Obama has mastered the skill of floating over Congress or the Constitution when either one gets in his way. He always stings America in the butt with whatever agenda he has dreamed up. Obama wants to **REPLACE** our founding principles with some hodgepodge that he and his buddies at Columbia have concocted. What we need is a president who will **REAPPLY** those principles. Obama's thought process is flawed from the start. He apparently believes that Madison went to the extreme in enunciating the principles of limited government. Further, Obama must disagree with Jefferson who believed that government exists not to **give rights** to the people, but to **protect and sustain those rights**, especially those that pre-date government. Obama preaches that we live in an enlightened age. His thinking that he is the light mars that thought process. Someone should point out to Mr. Obama that God is sovereign. He is still on the throne, and He can bring down emperors, czars, despots, and tyrants without consulting with an electoral college or big money men in America. If we, as Americans, are to regain faith in America, we must first return to a faith in the God who made America possible regardless of which party is in control of the White House.

We do not live in an "enlightened age." In spite of all the dazzling light produced by our nuclear power, we are once again living in the dark. Our society is living in the dark because we have dethroned the King of Light and replaced him with a prince of darkness. Scripture says that man prefers darkness rather than light, to hide our evil deeds. On one occasion during a church service that Obama was attending, some members of the clergy and certain choir members saw a beam of light pierce a stained glass window and illuminate Obama's face. They interpreted this as a divine revelation that he must be "the one." Let me straighten you out on this one, Pal. That was an optical illusion like all the other smoke and mirror illusions which this man has tried to slip by us like a Houdini magic trick. No, my Friend, the light has not yet shined upon Obama. His darkest secrets are yet to be unveiled. Obama is still practicing one of our early government's tactics-The "L. S. D. Tactic." (That is "lie,""steal" and "deceive.)" Early politicians were so good at L.S.D that the Indians accused them on many occasions of speaking with "forked tongues." Most of our present day politicians including Mr. Obama are masters of this tactic. They not only speak fluently with forked tongue, but also speak "forked- tongue" in several languages. Some go beyond this and speak in unknown tongues that no one can interpret. Just listen to some of Joe Biden's speeches or former President George W. Bush's speeches to understand what I mean.

The intensity of this darkness pervading our society is evident in the moral corruption of our culture. Evidence of the extensive power of the prince of darkness is witnessed in the dastardly deeds done by the likes of Jeffery Dalmer, and recently by the Batman Killer, James Holmes, not to mention the murder of thousands of babies each year in abortion clinics. Reading the daily news or turning on the TV exposes a tsunami of crime and corruption destroying America. The grim fact is that nothing surprises us. We have gotten comfortable in the dark. Sadly, we accept as normal all the dark and perverse evils without a word of protest.

Lot, we are told, was a righteous man, but he made a very bad decision. He saw that the grass appeared to be greener in Sodom so he moved his family downtown. At first no doubt, his soul was troubled by the ungodly things he saw in that wicked city. But slowly, like a frog put in warm water, he got used to it. By the time he realized that the water was boiling, it was too late. He lost his family and died in disgrace because he preferred the darkness over the light. "As it was in the days of Lot; even so shall it be in the day when the Son of Man is revealed." (Luke 17:28) We are living in a twenty-first century Sodom. We must quickly turn on the light. We must take the Light of the World from under the bushel where our government has hidden Him and give Him the crown and scepter which He rightfully deserves. Obama is not the light of the world. He is not the king. Elvis was not the king. Jesus Christ is King! As John Hagee so often says, "We better give Him praise and glory in the church and acknowledge Him in our nation."

Being satisfied with darkness does not happen all at once but comes slowly, imperceptibly. The poet Alexander Pope aptly describes the process, "Vice is a monster of such frightful mien, as to be hated, needs but to be seen; yet seen too oft, familiar with her face, we first endure, then pity, then embrace." We must choose between light or darkness, love or hate, sin or the savior, greed or grace. We cannot serve two masters. Our common sense course of action, given the extreme darkness, is clearly outlined for us in Ephesians 5:11; "And have no fellowship with the unfruitful works of darkness but, rather, reprove them." We must reprove the darkness of our nation's capital and replace it with the light of the world. We will never experience peace in our hearts, peace in our country, or peace in the world until the Prince of Peace is once again put on the throne. Thomas Paine told the early Americans the same thing about usurping the crown of England. He convinced most of the people that nearly all the problems tormenting their everyday lives and making it nearly impossible to make a living, were a direct result of swearing allegiance to the wrong king. We are in the same sinking Titanic. We too are burdened by ungodly and unnecessary taxes. We too must rebel against a government that has grown too big and too powerful. We must realize that a government, too large and controlling, stifles ambition and initiative by penalizing success. We too must regain our fundamental rights and freedoms.

Consider how truly blessed we are in America. Every American can worship at the church of his choice and serve the God of his choice. Most Americans have jobs that insure their families will not be hungry. Most Americans can pursue whatever level of education they desire. If your refrigerator is full and you have at least two suits of clothes, a roof over your head, and a safe place to sleep, you are wealthier than seventy-five percent of the world's population. But all this could change, and change very rapidly. With a few swift and thoughtless strokes of the presidential pen, Obama could destroy a lot of the things that we Americans hold dear. I do not pretend to know his complete agenda or all the plans he has for America. However, I have seen enough to know that whatever he has up his sleeve is not good for our country.

UNSAFE AUTOS AND UNSCRUPULOUS PRESIDENTS MUST BE RECALLED.

I would like to end this chapter with just a few of the endless reasons why Obama must not be allowed to complete the destruction of America. Obama's lies transcend space and time. This means that I have neither space nor time in which to list all of his campaign promises which turned out to be nothing but "whistling in the wind." He can manufacture lies at about the same rate that the Ford Motor Company can manufacture automobiles, sometimes even faster than a burger flipper can flip McDonald's hamburgers. We are all accustomed to politicians promising choice rib-eye during campaigns and delivering bologna once in office. However, he said he was different and things would change in America if he were elected. Things changed all right.... for the worse! The main thing that has really changed over the last few years has been the weather. We have had more hot air than ever before; the source being the White House. Listing just a few of the blatant lies told to the American people should ignite Americans to respond by demanding this "Presidential pretender" be removed from office. Please understand that this list is not exhaustive or complete.

Mr. Obama lied about his willingness to work with both political parties in Washington D.C. He is in fact the most partisan president that ever graced the Green Room (I assume they have a green room at the White House). Not only does he want the Democrats to win, he wants the Republicans to lose. He got his nice new house but let thousands of poor and middle class Americans lose theirs. An excerpt from 2008 Barack Obama campaign literature states, "Barack Obama will repeal this provision so that ordinary families can also get the relief that bankruptcy laws were intended to provide." At the beginning of 2008, thousands of homes were being foreclosed. Obama promised to swoop in like a Crimson Tide football player and tackle this problem. The Chapter 13 bankruptcy law prevents judges from altering the terms of home mortgages for ordinary families regardless of whether the loans were predatory, unfair, or otherwise, unaffordable. However, investors who own multiple homes and people with vacation homes can renegotiate those mortgages in bankruptcy court. Obama promised to change those laws in order to save thousands of homes for thousands of working class Americans. During the first year of Obama's administration, foreclosures continued to escalate. Obama did nothing to repeal the bankruptcy laws as promised.

Senator Obama vowed to come in like Mr. Clean and sterilize the ethical corruption that he claimed existed in previous administrations. His words were, "I promise to create a centralized internet database of lobbying reports, ethics records, and campaign finance filings." He also stated something about fighting for the establishment of an independent agency to oversee the investigations of congressional ethics violations. He kept his pledge to get rid of some of the evil lobbyists that hang out at D.C. A whole gaggle of these lobbyists now have different jobs. They now serve as members of Obama's cabinet and fill positions in other administrative roles. Need I say more?

Obama has been about as effective at securing our borders against illegal aliens as Jim Bowie was at keeping the Mexicans out of the Alamo. His campaign promise was, "I promise lasting and dedicated security to our borders and to do a better job patrolling the Canadian and Mexican borders." Once in office he maintained an ongoing stance against funding for a border fence. National Guard numbers on the southern border of the U.S. have been reduced by over sixty-five percent since he took office. At present, we still have over 1000 miles of uncontrolled borders while he continues to push amnesty for illegal immigrants so that he and the Democratic Party will have a continuous supply of loyal voters.

U-turns are illegal in most cases and present driving hazards. Mr. Obama evidently has no problem making a U-turn when it is expedient for him. As a senator Barack was crowing from one of his fence-posts about out of control congressional spending. During a speech on March 16th, 2006, he rebuked his congressional colleagues for wanting to raise the debt ceiling. He further stated that it was a sign of poor leadership for our elected officials to even consider a measure that would put such a heavy burden on our children and grandchildren. ***Warning U-turn Ahead***! Obama reminds me of a red-neck, beer-drinking deer hunter I once knew. He never had a secure job or steady income, yet he always had money for beer and bullets. He would chastise his wife if she spent too much money at the grocery store for essentials, but it was O.K. for him to spend any amount necessary for camouflaged shirts, deer-stands, and rifle scopes. Obama's most obvious mission since taking over the Oval Office has been to raise the debt limit to fund his special programs.

A "to" and "fro" motion is a desirable trait for a pendulum, but it is most unbecoming and hypocritical for a president. What did Illinois Senator Barack Obama have to say about gay marriages? "I favor legalizing same-sex marriages and would fight efforts to prohibit such marriages." What did President Obama say as he addressed this issue? "I believe marriage is between a man and a woman. I am not in favor of gay marriage." (From a campaign speech in 2008) The pendulum continues, "My opinion on gay marriage is evolving." (President Obama, speaking to a group of gay activists) My only comment here is, "Mr. President, we don't have time or patience for this Darwinian process to complete itself in your life." Where the pendulum stops, my friends, is simple. Follow the money. Find the pot of gold, and you will see the end of Obama's evolution on this matter. Regardless of how you feel about gay marriage, the larger and more important question is, "Can we trust a president who has more moves than a grandfather clock's pendulum?"

Obama is a political switch-hitter. This enhances his ability to deceive the American people. If you asked the average citizen whether or not a switch-hitter would have a higher batting average in a typical season than a one-way hitter, most Americans would answer, "Yes, the switch-hitter would probably have a higher batting average." Well, it is like Daniel Moynihan said, "we are entitled to our own opinions, but not to our own facts." Mickey Mantle's highest seasonal average of .365 was considerably lower than the highest average of a one-way hitter in the same time period. Obama's rhetoric constitutes his vain attempt to convince the taxpayers that his programs are working by merely changing his stance at the plate. No matter what spin Obama puts on tax or economic statistics, his batting average on all the important issues is embarrassingly dismal.

Obama's foreign policy is really scary. He has taken a position that is apparently "anti-Israel." The God of the universe has made it crystal clear that Israel is His favorite child. "For thus says the Lord of Hosts, He sent me after glory to the nations which plunder you; for he who touches you, touches the apple of His eye." (Zechariah 2:8) Anatomically, the "apple" is the pupil of the eye and the most sensitive part of the human body. What Zechariah is saying here is that anyone who attacks Israel or hurts them in any way is thrusting a finger into God's eye. God Himself is very protective of his favorite child. The Psalmist wrote, "He who keeps Israel shall neither slumber nor sleep." (Psalms 121:4) God has entered into many covenants in the Bible not the least of which is His covenant with the nation Israel through Abraham, the father of that nation. Listen to the incredible promise that God gave to Abraham, "I will bless those who bless you, and I will curse them who curse you, and in you, all the families of the earth shall be blessed." (Genesis 12:3) America needs the favor of God more than anything else in this universe today. The surest way to obtain that favor is to stand with the nation Israel and the Jewish people in their times of need. Regardless of how many nuclear weapons of mass destruction that we might have stockpiled and regardless of how clever our economic policies might be, the smartest, most common-sense course of action Americans can take as a nation is to align ourselves with Israel. End of story! Obama better read Jewish history to see how time after time God has honored His covenant and protected His people, utterly destroying those who would attack them.

Obama's ineptitude concerning foreign policy really becomes apparent when you consider the lack of military protection for our ambassadors who are often in harm's way. Evidently, he was not aware that extra security had been requested in Benghazi. Perhaps he was too busy campaigning to be concerned with such trivial matters. Surely we have enough intelligence to anticipate a terrorist attack on the anniversary of the 9/11 attack. If he was not aware that additional security had been requested, he should have been. The American people, including the dead ambassador's family, were kept in the dark for over two weeks following the terrorist hostility while the Obama regime figured out a politically correct excuse for the American deaths. Clearly, getting re-elected, in my opinion, was more important to Obama than the security of Chris Stevens and the other Americans who lost their lives in this episode of terrorism. It is ridiculous that the mainstream media made a big deal over the absurd allegations that Mitt Romney was responsible for the death of a woman after leaving Bain Capital, but is strangely silent concerning the actual deaths of four Americans in Libya. The best Obama has done concerning this debacle is to say, "I am truly sorry for the loss of American lives, we will fix it." How will he fix it? Is he going to use his messianic powers and resurrect the dead? Unfortunately Mr. Obama is not a handy-man. He is about as useful around the house (The white house) as Dagwood Bumstead was around his house. He has not fixed anything yet-and will not be able to fix the deaths in Libya. Arresting and punishing the perpetrators of this terrorism will not bring Chris Stephens back to life.

Not only is Obama turning a deaf ear to Israel but also he is turning a blind eye to the constitution of the United States. Listen to candidate Barack Obama, "The president does not have the power under the constitution, to unilaterally authorize a military attack in a situation that does not involve stopping an actual or imminent threat to the nation." Obama has been very outspoken and critical of the Bush Administration for the Iraq and Afghanistan wars. He painted his predecessors as war-mongering abusers of the constitution and himself as a shining knight whose foreign policies would be "by the book" so to speak. Here is the fact. Obama announced all of a sudden that U.S. planes had begun bombing Libya. THIS WAS DONE WITHOUT CONGRESSIONAL CONSENT!

This action is a complete reversal of his campaign promise. This military operation did not involve stopping an imminent threat to America. Common sense conclusion—true to his character, Obama lied.

I could give you vast evidence of broken promises and lies. I am buried in stacks of congressional records, campaign speeches, and internet clips, documenting the sad and twisted story of a president who needs recalling worse than a Ford with dangerous steering problems. Please feel free to call me for more documented Obama lies and failures to be true to the American people. Consider a final quote from one of America's best presidents, "You cannot bring about prosperity by discouraging thrift. You cannot strengthen the weak by weakening the strong. You cannot help the wage-earner by pulling down the wage-payer. You cannot further the brotherhood of man by encouraging class hatred. You cannot help the poor by destroying the rich. You cannot keep out of trouble by spending more than you earn. You cannot build character and courage by taking away man's initiative and independence. You cannot help men permanently by doing for them what they could and should do for themselves." (Abraham Lincoln)

I wonder if Obama or anyone in the Democratic Party has any idea of how many countries which tried to "spread the wealth" actually ended up spreading poverty. Obama needs to read history and the constitution before trying to impersonate an American president.

I cannot end my comments without addressing presidential debates. As an American citizen I am totally embarrassed with how some of the debates were conducted. I hope most children in America were busy with homework or already in bed during the debates. Children could not learn how to be adults by watching those fiascos. All they could learn were bad manners, violation of rules, and how to be a jackass if they watched Joe Biden in action. I have a couple of common-sense suggestions if we are to have presidential debates in the future. First, establish some clear-cut rules and find an impartial moderator with enough sense, intestinal fortitude, and power to control the participants in the debate and the spectators in the audience. I agree with Rush Limbaugh when he called Candy Crowley's performance "an act of terrorism." Some misguided anonymous writer hailing from Scripps Howard News Service said that Crowley deserved a medal. That is the most hilarious statement I have heard during the whole campaign. Most of the debates had about as much class and decorum as a women's mud-wrestling event sponsored by the Red-neck Women's Association. Second, the rules of the debate must be clearly explained to the contestants. They must be warned that the moderator will have absolute authority to enforce the rules. Let them know that they could get very humiliated by the sound of a loud buzzer interrupting them if they commit a foul. In future years, if technology provides the means, a lie detector and electric cow prod could be wired to each contestant. Contestants would receive a powerful jolt of electricity every time a blatant lie issued from their mouths. In this way, Americans could finally be assured that the truth was being told. Well, maybe not. The debate preparation teams would probably condition the contestants by intense shock tolerance training. Ability to lie with twenty volts of electricity flowing through your body would then become the number-one criteria for becoming a presidential candidate. Moderators should not only have absolute power to keep the candidates in line, but also have complete control over the audience. Michelle Obama committed the most uncultured, ill-mannered, and red-neck violation of decorum and protocol in the history of first ladies when she applauded for her husband during the second debate. She reminded me of a silly teen-ager cheering for her boy-friend after he won a teddy-bear at a carnival. This behavior shows the contempt that both Mr. and Mrs. Obama have for the rules by which everyone else has to play. They obviously think they are exceptions to the rules. Mrs. Obama's blatant disregard for the rules of the debate by leading a round of applause ranks up there with the embarrassing behavior of Billy Carter, the beer drinking brother of former President Jimmy Carter. Barack, you need to go on another apology tour. Instead of apologizing for the actions America takes while maintaining our freedoms, you should apologize to all Americans for your behavior the last four years and for your wife's behavior during the presidential debate.

No past president of the United States is more deserving of impeachment than Barack Obama. His excessive use of executive power and the many unconstitutional atrocities he has committed, head the list of reasons to impeach. He has wasted tons of green energy money, given away money to our enemies, and just lately given military aircraft and other weapons to the Muslim Brotherhood. He held a Muslim prayer meeting on the White House grounds, yet denied Americans a national day of prayer. He constantly tries to force homosexuality, same sex marriage, and abortion on America while the idea of God being put in the Democratic Platform was "booed" at the Democratic National Convention. In my opinion, the number one item on America's to-do list is to initiate impeachment proceeding before we let this Hitler-like radical destroy America.

Obama could have been a great president. I sincerely wanted him to be. I did not vote for him, but I got in his corner and tried to be a team player by praying for him. In fact, I think he wanted to be a good president at first, but he had an identity crisis. He never figured out who he was. He wanted to emulate Abraham Lincoln, even going so far as to launch his presidential campaign from the same steps in Springfield, Illinois as Lincoln did. He wanted to be like Jefferson and be a smart president. Unfortunately, he missed that mark too. I have never seen so much brain and so little common sense in the same cerebral cortex. He wanted to be like FDR and come up with programs that would put a chicken in every pot and a car in every garage. But, alas, like so many social programs that preceded it, Obama's did not work either. If only he had resolved to be himself and followed Shakespeare's advice, "To thine own self, be true." Think of what great things he could have accomplished as the first black president. If he had built on the foundation that our founding fathers established instead of trying to tear them down and start from scratch, he could have accomplished so much more. I think he could have made great strides in diminishing the race issues that still linger in America, but choosing to align himself with such radical extremists as Jeremiah Wright, and others, nipped that possibility in the bud. He could have solved many of our economic problems had he identified with the many poor and middle class workers in America and listened to advisors who knew a lot more than he did about how to stimulate a depressed economy. He could have saved a lot of American lives and billions of American dollars by getting our service men out of places where they do not belong in the first place. Instead, he sends more troops to yet more places, and does this without consent of congress. Why did he fail in all these areas and more? In my opinion, it is because he is a selfish individual who thinks not of the plight of future Americans, but only of the present and future of Barack Obama.

His many failures as president can also be attributed to the fact that his priorities have apparently always been out of order. One should not worry about draining the swamp or getting rid of mosquitoes when you are up to your neck in alligators. Obama reminds me of a rabid Alabama football fan who had two season-ticket seats on the fifty-yard line at Bryant-Denny Stadium. He was sitting alone at a game one cool, windy day in October. A guy way up in the cheap seats, having trouble seeing the game, spotted the empty seat and noted that it had been vacant almost the whole first quarter. He shuffled down there at the end of the first quarter and inquired about the empty seat. The man told him that it was his wife's seat but that she was deceased. The fellow asked him why he had not given the seat to a close friend or relative? The rabid Alabama fan replied, "They are all at the funeral, go ahead and have a seat if you like." As we review some of the decisions made by Obama during his first four years in office, we must conclude that his priorities are just as irresponsible and laughable.

AFTERWORD

In the first part of this book, I gave a bit of the history of our American Revolution. When you consider all the odds of America winning, you will have to agree that we either had an incredible run of good luck or some higher power was looking out for us. I think the success of the American Revolution can be summed up in two words: God and Unity. What thirteen individual colonies could never do separately, one unified nation could. What was impossible for a contingent of untrained, poorly armed farmers and merchants was possible with the help of God himself. Realizing that the 1700's America was a vast, sparsely settled country, early proponents of freedom created the "Sons of Liberty" and the "Committees of Correspondence" which linked the colonists together in a viable network. Helping in this unification process were fast-riding couriers like Paul Revere and William Dawes. Today, we have a much more efficient courier in the internet. I challenge each of you who want to preserve our American freedoms to ride this mighty steed and help educate each other about what is happening in America. Once alerted to the dangers we face as a nation, I am confident that Americans will rally together as they did at Independence Hall, Philadelphia and take appropriate actions to preserve our freedoms. I am not so concerned with whether you are a Democrat or Republican, a conservative or liberal. In other words, I am not concerned with where you stand, but which direction you will go, if, and when you move. What will you do? Will you come forward and speak out? The American Dream is still possible, but we must act now to preserve it for our children and grandchildren. Can't we come together as a united America as we did in 1776 and on 9/11/2001? Can we not have a great impact on the direction our country goes if we rally together? Are you willing to listen, to learn, and to lead? Others may follow, but they are waiting for you. They need an example to follow. A final question, "Will you move the boulder?"

In ancient times a king had a boulder placed on a roadway. Then he hid himself and watched to see if anyone would remove the huge rock. Some of the king's wealthiest merchants and courtiers came by and simply walked around it. Many loudly blamed the king for not keeping the roads clear, but none did anything about getting the stone out of the way. Finally, a peasant came along carrying a load of vegetables. Upon approaching the boulder, the peasant laid down his burden and tried to move the stone to the side of the road. After much pushing and straining, he finally succeeded. When the peasant picked up his load of vegetables, he noticed a purse lying in the road where the boulder had been. The purse contained many gold coins and a note from the king indicating that the gold was for the person who removed the boulder from the roadway. The peasant learned what many never understand. Every obstacle presents an opportunity to improve our condition. Every American has two choices: You can be part of the problem or part of the solution. You can continue to blame the government for the rocks in the road, or you can do your part to be a **"pebble pusher."**

ABOUT THE AUTHOR

Ken English is from the small south Alabama town of Gantt, Alabama. Ken is a distinguished honor graduate of Lurleen Wallace Jr. College in Andalusia, Alabama. He has a B.S. degree in biology and physical education and a M.S. degree in psychology from Troy University. Ken is a veteran high-school basketball coach of fifteen years. He has won numerous coaching awards including both football and basketball coach of the year awards in 1989.

After retiring from coaching, Ken became CEO of Superior Architectural Designs. In this capacity, Ken developed molds for mass production of various architectural components including columns and capitals of Greek and Roman orders.

Ken also does consulting for the restoration of historic landmarks and projects. The City of Enterprise commissioned Ken to make a life-size replica of the famous Boll Weevil monument. This statue is the pride and joy of the city of Enterprise. The sculpture was on display at the Atlanta History Museum during the 1992 Olympics.

In 2001, Ken, together with his son Kyle, started a new business enterprise- English Sculptures LLC. The company produces original works of art including historical, collegiate, and portrait sculptures. When not in his studio working on sculptures, Ken operates a two-hundred acre cattle ranch near Elba, Alabama.

Ken has been married to his wife, Patsy, since 1971. They have two children: Kyle and Jennifer—and six grand-children: Ayden, Skye, and Laken English, Davin, Dylan, and Daxton McCoy.

REFERENCES

1. Thomas Paine, *Common Sense,* (Dover Press, 1997)
2. Alan Axelrod, *Guide to the American Revolution,* (Alpha Books, 2000)
3. Kenneth E. Hamburger, Joseph R. Fischer, Steven C. Gravin, *Why America is Free,* (The Society of the Cincinnati, 1998)
4. Mike Huckabee, *A Simple Government,* (Sentinel Publications, 2011)
5. Jeff Rovin, *The Unbelievable Truth,* (The Penguin Group, 1994)
6. Dr. Max Rafferty, *Suffer Little Children,* (The Devin-Adair Co. 1963)
7. Max Rafferty, *Max Rafferty on Education,* (The Devin-Adair Co. 1968)
8. Dr. James Dobson, *Bringing up Boys,* (Tyndale House Publishers, 2001)
9. John Eidsmoe, *Christianity and the Constitution,* (Baker Book House Co. 1987)
10. Bob Schieffer, *Bob Shieffer's America,* (G.P. Putnam's Sons, 2008)
11. John Roger & Peter McWilliams, *Wealth 101,* (Prelude Press, 1992)
12. John Linder & Neal Boortz, *The Fair Tax Book,* (Harper Collins Publishers, 2005)
13. David Barton, *The Bulletproof Washington,* (Wallbuilder Press, 1990)
14. Ted Baehr & Susan Wales, *Faith in God and Generals,* (Broadman & Holman, 2003)
15. Bill O'Reilly, *The No Spin Zone,* (Broadway Books, 2001)
16. Anthony Holm, *52 Reasons Not to Vote for Obama,* (Mascot Books, 2012)
17. Edward Klein, *The Amateur,* (Regnery Publishing, Inc. 2012)
18. David Limbaugh, *The Great Destroyer,* (Regnery Publishing, 2012)
19. Adrian Rogers, *Kingdom Authority,* (Broadman & Holman, 2002)

www.ingramcontent.com/pod-product-compliance
Lightning Source LLC
Chambersburg PA
CBHW032026290526
45786CB00011B/569